STRETCHED HORIZONS

Ross Richdale

I0164837

When Sunset Grove Primary's Headteacher, Bree Ashworth goes to help teacher Jenny Dench in her classroom she is attacked by an intruder. The attacker escapes and Bree is taken to hospital. Her husband Colin arrives and tells her he is leaving to move from London with his mistress Linda Rouke.

Bree has bookings to attend a reading conference in New Zealand over that country's summer vacation. With double tickets bought and Colin gone, she invites Jenny to come with her.

In New Zealand, the small commuter aeroplane they fly in crashes in thick bush country. The pilot is killed and Jenny and Bree try to survive by themselves. However, all is not lost, for a tramper in the bush, Ray Barnett and his dog, Pattie find them.

Police in England tell Colin, Bree has been involved in an air crash and is missing. Colin abandons his partner and flies out to New Zealand but his intentions are not those one would expect from a worried husband....

PURRBOOKS

Copyright ©2005
Ross Richdale

All characters in this book have no existence outside the imagination of the author and have no relation to anyone bearing the same name or names. Any resemblance to individuals known or unknown to the author are purely coincidental.

National Library of New Zealand Cataloguing-in-Publication Data

Richdale, Ross, 1941-
Stretched horizons / Ross Richdale.
ISBN 0-95826-142-3
I. Title.
NZ823.3—dc 22

Cover design by Ross Richdale

Paperback published by

Purrbooks
Palmerston North
NEW ZEALAND

CHAPTER ONE

Headteacher Bree Ashworth yawned, gathered up an armful of folders and headed out her office door. Sunset Grove Primary had had more than the usual problems over the long exhausting week and there was still the PTFA meeting in two hours. As the attractive blonde woman headed through the empty outer office, a buzzer sounded.

She turned to see a red console light flashing. This alarm was activated by class teachers for emergencies and came from the Badger Room, Jenny Dench's Year One class. Bree frowned. Jenny Dench was the youngest teacher on the staff but was also the daughter of her parents' friends from way back.

Why was Jenny still in the building? It was after five and the caretaker should have locked up by now. Perhaps there was another short-circuit. The new system had had more than its fair share of teething problems.

In one deft movement, she turned on the television surveillance system and pressed button twenty-three. It flicked alive, and Jenny's screams vibrated from the speakers.

"Oh my...!" Bree gasped. The folders in her arms fluttered to the ground.

A man was in the room, attacking Jenny. Even it those few microseconds Bree saw Jenny slumped backward over her desk, kicking and shrieking as a man wrestled with her. Bree hit another emergency button, hoped the caretaker was still on the premises, and headed outside.

She ran along the corridor and headed upstairs to the Top Hall. Trust Jenny's room to be one of the farthest away! To her relief, the Top Hall lights blazed. She could see Badger Room Door leading off the opposite side.

The screams and thumps reached her senses first. Without really thinking of any consequences, she tore in the room. Jenny was pinned back over her desk with her skirt hauled up, her stockinged feet kicking into the air. Her shrieks had changed to almost inaudible sobs.

"Perhaps next time you might..." the attacker snarled.

Jenny managed to wriggle an arm free and gouge her fingernails down the man's face. Blood oozed from the wound but this only made him more violent. He slapped her face with so much force she staggered sideways and crashed onto the floor.

"Leave her alone!" Bree screamed. She launched her slender frame at the man and managed to topple him sideways away from Jenny. The petrified younger woman crawled away, but Bree had more immediate problems. The attacker turned and, with one almighty swing of his arm, knocked her sideways onto a floor mat. Before she could stagger to her knees, heavy work boots kicked out.

His leg movement was a blur; Bree felt a sharp pain in her ribs and gasped in agony as she crashed sideways over one of the Year One tables. Another kick grazed off her head. She screamed at the excruciating pain, but managed to roll sideways to fend off the third kick.

The man sniggered. "So, Headteacher Bree Ashworth is about to meet her maker."

Bree could see grinning lips and eyes totally devoid of empathy. The man lunged at her but she anticipated the movement, pulled back and pushed a child's table between them. The man flung the table aside and grabbed her hair, pulled her head back and squeezed her throat.

Her despair turned to utter terror when she couldn't breathe. A chuckle filled the air. He was enjoying himself!

The room spun and her vision blurred as she tried to swallow. She had almost lost consciousness when an object flew across her vision. A heavy mop hit the intruder across his body. Her attacker staggered back and released the pressure on her throat. His arm came up but the mop swung a second time and sent him careering across the carpet. A thickset man dived at the would-be rapist but the element of surprise was over. Spluttering, and with tears pouring down her cheeks, Bree managed to crawl further away between two more tables. She pulled herself up and saw John, the caretaker, run towards the door in pursuit of the man who had attacked them.

She attempted to speak but purple clouds enveloped her and she sank, unconscious, to the floor.

*

It was the unusual smell that tickled Bree's senses even before she opened her eyes, that antiseptic smell of enforced cleanliness along with the more pleasant aroma of roses. She felt crisp material touching her, something itching at her nose and the sensation of numbness across her lower body. Jarring pain shot across her ribs. The voice came through a fog. She thought she should know it.

"Bree, are you awake?"

Bree couldn't fathom why was she lying down. There was the PTFA meeting to attend. Someone had filed a complaint about the cost of lunches going up twenty pence and the blandness of meals being offered. She smiled. Of course, something like lunches would attract far more parents than if they were having a discussion about the new reading program.

"Oh, Bree, please wake up," Jenny's voice pleaded. "You saved me, you know. He would have raped me. Now, you have to suffer.... The bastard took off when John arrived... "

Bree opened her eyes to see Jenny staring at her across a hospital room. "Where am I?" she muttered.

"Oh, thank God, you're awake. I'll ring for the nurse."

Bree managed a smile. "No, wait a moment. Oh my..." The memories returned with everything in stark detail. She attempted to sit up but her ribs were too painful. Her head spun but she was determined to stay conscious. "Jenny," she said. "Was I in time?"

The young woman opposite her blinked back tears and wiped a blackened eye. She nodded. "And I was one who reckoned the new surveillance system was a waste of money."

"And how are you?"

"Not as bad as you. Bruises and scratches. My confidence is shot to hell, though. How could the bastard? He said he was Jamie Hargraves' father. Like an idiot, I believed him..." Jenny's lips quivered. She shuddered and blew her nose. "The doctor reckoned the kick on the side of the head knocked you out. They've admitted you overnight just in case something goes wrong."

Bree felt a heavy bandage around her head and another across her chest. She glanced around. "I guess I've been out for a while? Where did you say we were?"

Jenny gave one of her famous little giggles. "I didn't, but we're in the Charing Cross Hospital. We been here almost an hour."

"How's John?"

"A reluctant hero. You know how modest he is? The guy who attacked us ran across the Top Hall and down the back stairs. John was all ready to run after him but I screamed to let him go."

"So, it wasn't Jamie's father?"

Jenny shook her head. "No, the police followed that lead up. Jamie's father looks nothing like him. I was a cot case, blubbering like a baby, and the doctor told them to come back."

"Don't run yourself down, Jenny," Bree said. She gazed further around the room. There was a huge teddy bear propped up on the windowsill. She wriggled over to reach for it but felt queasy and collapsed back on her pillow.

"I'll get the nurse." Jenny's determined voice cut in through the haze.

*

Morning came, with Jenny arriving even before the police. Detective Constable Margaret Blackburn, who accompanied a uniformed constable, said they were following leads but nobody had been arrested.

"We'll follow up Miss Dench's information about the attacker's knowledge of one of your pupils. It appears to be someone who picked her at random, though. We've had cases of men hanging around primary schools before. The young teachers and mothers can be an attraction if a man is that way inclined." Constable Blackburn turned to Jenny. "Can you remember seeing the man any time before the attack, perhaps watching you cross the road, getting into your car or during an outing?"

Jenny frowned. "He looked a typical parent, was clean-shaven and wore a new suit..." She stopped and bit on her lip. "The funny thing is, I think I've seen him before."

"Where?"

"I can't remember. We meet so many parents and others on sports days and so forth. I don't think he was a parent of any of my pupils, though."

"Okay," Detective Constable Blackburn replied. "We'll get a more formal statement from both of you later."

Bree nodded.

"Meanwhile, if you remember anything, no matter how insignificant, just jot it down. If this is the person we're looking for, it may solve a number of similar attacks."

"Other teachers?" Bree asked.

"All work related places with a high ratio of female employees, Mrs. Ashworth. Several were in office buildings and all were when the victim was alone after hours in their own supposedly safe environment." The DC smiled slightly. "We believe this man didn't know about your surveillance monitors."

"They've only been in for three weeks," Bree replied

"That's interesting. Perhaps the attack was planned well in advance."

"He knew I was the headteacher and even called me by name," Bree added.

DC Blackburn frowned. "And you've never seen him before?"

"It's hard to remember. I doubt if I'd recognise him. I only really saw him from the side. It all happened so quickly."

The constable smiled and shut her notebook. "Thank you both," she said. "We'll be in touch."

*

Only moments after the police left another visitor arrived. Bree sighed.

"Rushing into things without thinking of the consequences again, Bree," the man said. "You're damn lucky the caretaker arrived."

"Hello, Colin," Bree replied without enthusiasm. She turned to Jenny. "This is my husband, Colin."

Jenny frowned and muttered a greeting.

"So, the trip will have to go," Colin said, after Bree gave him a brief explanation of what happened. "We'll lose the deposit but I'll cancel the tickets."

Bree's eyes fluttered with the first signs of emotion. "I'd still like to go," she whispered. "You know I've been asked to speak at the conference."

Colin glanced away. "There's been a change of plans. I was going to tell you anyway," he muttered.

"Tell me what?" Bree felt indignant.

"I've accepted that position in Birmingham. They want me to start at the beginning of next month."

"Well, I'm not going," Bree snapped. "I am not about to give up my position to follow you around the country, Colin. We've been through all that. I've done it before. No more..." Her eyes flashed. "...And I thought a holiday would help patch our marriage up," she added in a whisper.

Colin shrugged. "I tried," he whispered.

"Sure," Bree's voice rose an octave as thoughts came to the forefront of her mind. Who was it that turned a blind eye when Colin never arrived home at night, and during those business weekends over to the eastern seaboard? Who pretended she never noticed that his secretary was also out of town at the same time? Their marriage has been a sham for years now. She was just a suitable person to have at his social functions. If Jenny wasn't present she'd tell him that, too! Instead, she swallowed and glanced away. "And what about Linda Rouke?" she muttered.

Colin Ashworth ignored Bree but switched his eyes to Jenny. However, the flush on his cheeks did not pass unnoticed. "I'm sorry to hear of this attack, Miss Dench," he said. "I'm glad your caretaker arrived in time." His eyes switched back. "We'll talk later, Bree," he said. "Take care. 'Bye." He walked out without even a backward glance.

"Cold fish," Jenny said.

"Yeah," Bree replied.

"Who's Linda Rouke?"

Bree felt emotions rise through her body. "She was his secretary and they had an affair. She's moved up a notch to become his full time mistress. She recently transferred to Birmingham and I'm pretty sure he's set up a flat there for her." She attempted to remain calm. "His job takes him across there all the time." She turned. "That's the trouble with teaching, isn't it?"

"What do you mean, Bree?"

"It takes a total commitment and doesn't allow for personal circumstances. Colin is into the business circuit. Everything went well when I was the sexy, young wife to parade around. However, when I became a deputy, he changed." Bree shrugged. "I thought he'd be proud of me but the opposite happened. It was almost as if I was a competitor. It became worse when I moved to my present position as headteacher at Sunset Grove."

"Chauvinistic pig," Jenny replied.

"Exactly."

"And that holiday?"

"I've been invited to talk at an international reading conference in January. I was looking forward to swimming in the ocean on New Year's Day."

"Midwinter! Where, Australia?"

Bree smiled. "Well, you aren't far out. New Zealand, actually. It'll be midsummer there and the conference is during their summer holidays. Colin had agreed to come as it tied-in with some takeover bid his firm is involved in down there."

Jenny nodded. "So, it's all off. A pity. After all this, a good holiday away is what you need."

"You, too," Bree replied. "Why don't you come to New Zealand with me?"

"Me?" Jenny laughed. "My God, I've only been out of the country once and that was only a weekend in France." She shrugged. "I couldn't afford the aeroplane tickets let alone accommodation and other expenses. Newly graduated teachers don't get paid a lot, you know."

*

Bree was discharged from hospital that afternoon with a whole weekend ahead. She braced herself for a final confrontation with Colin but it never eventuated. When he didn't answer her phone call, she took a taxi home and found the place empty. Colin was gone, as was everything even remotely connected to his half of the community property. Clothes, tools, one television, the main computer and even one of their bed sets were gone.

"The bastard," Bree muttered as she walked through the house. The new washer, only purchased a month back, had gone. In its place, the old one was reconnected to the water supply.

In the kitchen, she picked up a brown envelope. Inside was a formal inventory of what Colin had taken, and a terse letter. Tears brimming her eyes, she read it. He was so thorough that he'd even left a cheque to pay for the month's electricity, groceries and other domestic expenses.

She continued to the last paragraph.

You'll find I have closed our joint account. Don't worry, half the amount in it has been deposited in your own account. As for the trip, I never cancelled the tickets. You can have them to do with as you wish. As you know, my lawyer is...

Bree stopped reading, placed the letter back in the envelope, sat down and wept. This was so typical of the man. He was too cowardly to confront her face to face and the one time she could do with a little warmth and understanding, he up and left. Well, Linda Rouke could have him. She could flutter her eyebrows at his customers and pamper to his tastes until he became tired of her and found a new mistress.

Bree sat staring into space and almost missed the light tap on the outside door. It was Jenny.

"Hi," Jenny said. "There's nobody home and I couldn't stand being in my flat by myself so I...." She stopped and stared. "What's wrong, Bree?"

Bree sighed. "Does it look so obvious?"

"It's more than your bruises and bandages. You look as white as a ghost."

"Come in," Bree responded. "I'm glad you dropped in. How'd you like a drink?"

"Cup of tea?"

"No," Bree replied. "I was thinking more of a stiff brandy. Bet the old bastard took all the liquor, too." She laughed sarcastically. "No, he'd have left each bottle half full."

"What is it, Bree?"

"Colin's left," Bree whispered. "He took half of everything, too. It's a wonder the bastard didn't rip our sheets in half." She took the envelope from the table and handed it to her visitor. "Have a read if you wish."

Jenny nodded and read the long-winded note.

"Well, you're best off without him," she finally said. "What a time to do it, though."

CHAPTER TWO

With the busy final weeks of the term at Sunset Grove, conversation about the attack on two of its teachers dropped. Other items rose to the fore, and life returned to normal. Except for Jenny and Bree.

Bree immersed herself in work, but did not miss the fact that Jenny had withdrawn. The young teacher no longer visited the staff lounge after school, no longer chatted with the other teachers, no longer participated. Worse, her famous giggle had disappeared. Bree decided to take action. She called Jenny in for a conference.

One of the tasks Bree did during the last two weeks was to hold an informal interview with each staff member. Here, they'd discuss anything the teacher wished about their class, and children, parents or school life in general. The ones Bree had held the term before were somewhat formal, with teachers feeling apprehensive and often on defence. However, this time the meetings were relaxed and gave the staff a chance to air items in privacy. They trusted Bree now and knew any comments or criticisms would not go beyond the office walls.

During these interviews Bree found there was deep interest in her own welfare. Staff members asked how she was coping after her marriage dissolved. Several offered suggestions and supported her decision to still go on her New Zealand holiday. Also, Bree discovered that most staff members noticed Jenny's change in behaviour with concern. Several had tried to help the young teacher, but to no avail.

After morning recess, a relieving teacher took the Year Ones in Badger Room while Jenny went into Bree's office for her interview. She looked pale and appeared timid and formal.

"I'm sorry about the class, Bree," Jenny blurted out before the headteacher had even sat down. "They've been quite naughty and it's all my fault. I'm sure Joan has already...." Joan was the manager of the Set One Classes.

"I've spoken to Joan," Bree replied, calmly. "She said she is proud of your efforts. Your planning and record keeping is suburb, parent interviews were thoroughly researched and everything is carried out professionally."

"But what about Mrs. Flores?" Jenny bit on her lip.

"Mary Flores has three children at this school. She complains about every teacher, every year." Bree smiled. "Frankly, if she hadn't mumbled about her little Christopher in your room, I would have wondered what was wrong. Next time, just refer her on to me. We have an understanding. She moans on and I ignore her. The poor lady is quite lonely, you know."

"I know, but..." Without warning, Jenny broke down into shuddering sobs. Her body trembled and, for a few moments, she just sat on her chair, unable to control her emotions. Finally, she stood and headed for the door. Bree stopped her, and Jenny huddled in her arms, sobbing.

"Here," Bree said a moment later and handed Jenny a tissue. "Just let it all come out. Don't hold back. I understand." She smiled softly. "I was there. Remember?"

"I know. Perhaps you're the only one who does understand, but it doesn't seem to affect you, Bree."

"It doesn't? Then perhaps you could explain why I've spent nearly every night since Colin left sleeping with a light left on?"

Jenny stopped sobbing, stepped back and wiped her eyes. "You have?"

"Yes," Bree whispered. "It's so silly but the house I've lived in for over a decade has suddenly started to make strange noises. I reckon I hear every creak and groan of the timbers. Colin was a ripe pain in the butt but he was always there or returning soon. Now, I wake up in the middle of the night covered in sweat and can feel the monster's boot kick me in the ribs."

Jenny whispered. "Me, too, but you're always so self-assured."

"A facade I've built up, Jenny. In my position, it's necessary. I've just used it a little more often in the last couple of weeks, that's all."

Jenny smiled through her tears. "I've always aspired to a position like yours. Fat lot of good I'd be at helping others when the first little thing that goes wrong makes me collapse in self-pity like a pack of cards."

"It wasn't little, and I believe you're coping well."

"Until now."

"Not necessarily. It's harder to talk about these things than to try to bury them in the back of your mind."

Jenny grinned. "My God, we're talking in clichés aren't we?"

"It makes what I'm going to say easier, though."

Jenny's eyes widened and her face paled. "Go on," she stuttered.

"Oh, it's nothing bad. You know all about the holiday Colin and I planned?"

"Sure."

"I can't cancel half a ticket. To re-book it for one costs more than I'd save, so I thought you might like to come with me."

"Bree, I'd love to, but I can't afford it. Anyhow, I'm not really into swimming."

Bree held up her arm. "I doubt if I can manage much swimming either. I'd still like to go for a dive in the ocean on New Year's Day just to say I've done it. I've managed to get the itinerary changed in New Zealand. Instead of pre-booked accommodation at the flash resort hotels Colin likes, I've booked into family motels. We can hire a car and go wherever we please."

"Damn, Bree. If I had the money..."

"You only need living expenses. Think of it as Colin's shout. The bastard owes me that much. If I go alone it will cost exactly the same amount. Besides, I'd like your company." She held another tissue out to her assistant, who was on the verge of tears again.

"But of all the people you could choose..."

"Stop arguing, Miss Dench. The offer's there. Do you want to come or not?" Bree's attempt at being formal faltered when she had to smile.

"How can I turn down a direct request from my Headteacher?" Jenny said. "My God, I haven't even got a passport, I'll need a new summer clothes and..."

"It's four weeks away," Bree cut in. "I'm sure all that can be sorted out."

"Thanks, Bree," Jenny replied. She gave Bree a tight hug before she glanced at her watch. "Damn, I need to get back to my room." She blew her nose and wiped her moist cheeks. "You're one in a million," she said and headed for the door.

"Another cliché, Miss Dench. You must try to be more original."

Jenny smiled. "Yes, Headteacher," she said, gave a mock salute and disappeared.

Bree glanced at her appointment book. Oh my, the next interview was with Jocelyn Hamilton, the one staff member who needed massive amounts of guidance, not that she would accept any. It was time to pull rank.

*

During the final week of the term Jenny almost became her old self again. The giggles and comical interruptions returned to the staff meetings, and she was there every afternoon.

"I reckon I'll buy my swimwear down there," she said to Bree one evening when she called around with a pile of pamphlets and books about New Zealand. "The whole country has a population a quarter of London's. I got a New Zealand Herald out at the airport. I thought their clothes were expensive until I realized one pound is over three dollars."

"It's one of the great outdoor tourist resorts of the world with mountains, lakes and geysers, as well as beaches," Bree added. "Well, that's what the brochures say."

Jenny giggled, unfolded a map onto the carpet and knelt down in front of it. "I got my passport," she said. "Told them there was a family emergency and I needed it straight right away." She glanced up and saw Bree's raised eyebrows. "Well, it is, isn't it? We had the emergency. I just forgot to tell them it happened here."

"Oh, Jenny," Bree said with a laugh. "I don't think we'll be bored down there, not even for a minute."

*

Ray Barnett was in the waiting room in one of the new sections of the hospital, a room with comfortable armchairs, low tables and assorted magazines spread around. The receptionist's counter was empty, as staff had since gone home. Three people were in the room - a couple in their sixties, and a man a generation younger, who endlessly strutted around. He stopped by a vertical goldfish bowl to gaze at the tiny creatures frolicking around in the artificial light, before running a hand over his day old stubble and continuing his relentless pace.

"Come and sit down, Ray," the woman said. "Can I get you another coffee from the dispensing machine?"

"Damn windows," the man replied. "Why don't they have windows in the place?"

"Something to do with the cost of making them earthquake proof," the third person in the room, a grey-headed man, replied. "It was cheaper to leave them out."

Ray's eyes were haunted and a vein in his neck twitched. "Sure, Ken," he said and switched the conversation back to what was really in his mind. "Why are they so long? They said midnight at the outside." He glanced at a clock on the wall that showed it was two-fifteen.

"Can we both have a coffee, Emily?" Ray's father-in-law Ken Preston said softly and walked over to comfort him.

"I'm sorry," Ray muttered. "I know it is just as difficult for you two, probably more so. After all, Maxine is your daughter. I've only known her for a decade." He acknowledged the hand on his shoulder with a faint smile and allowed himself to be guided into an armchair.

Ray's mother-in-law returned with two paper cups of coffee. She handed them out and Ray met her eyes.

"Thank you," she whispered. "Whatever happens tonight, I want you to know you were the best thing that happened to Maxie..." Her own voice broke and she turned away.

Another quarter an hour slipped by before an end door swung open and a nurse dressed in operating fatigues entered. Her body language told the grim story before she even opened her mouth.

"Doctor Mansfield will speak to you in a moment, Mr. Barnett," she said.

Ray stood and stared. "My wife...."

"I'm sorry," the nurse continued. "Maxine died on the operating table at two-forty three, five minutes ago. Doctor Mansfield will be here soon."

The hushed room was cut by sobs as Emily broke down. Ray fought his own emotions as he watched Ken clasp Emily in his arms.

"Thank you," Ray replied. "We knew it was a long shot, and I'm sure you all did everything possible." Without another word he walked out of the room.

*

Ray watched Emily tip the bucket of dirty water down the sink and stand back to check the last cleaning up of the empty house. In the six months since Maxie's funeral, Ray had taken it hard. His in-laws had tried to persuade him to stay in Auckland but he'd made up his mind to accept a position to survey noxious weed spread in native forests three hundred kilometres away in the southern part of the North Island. He reasoned that this position gave him a chance to follow up his botany degree knowledge. Really it was just an excuse to move away from his memories. Perhaps he'd get it out of his system and return sometime. The home that he and Maxie had lived in for five years was sold and the furniture had already gone south to where he'd bought another property.

"An empty house loses its soul, doesn't it, Ray?" Emily interrupted his thoughts.

"The house lost it when Maxie went," Ray replied. "I thought I could cope, but the memories are too vivid. I must move on before I wallow in self pity and become embittered."

"But you can come back," Emily said. "Our home is always open for you, whether it's just for a weekend or for a longer term." Ray noticed her compassionate gaze. "Keep in touch, won't you?"

Ray nodded. "I will," he whispered. "You're my only family now." He stepped forward, wrapped his arms around her chubby body and kissed on her cheek. "Well, I'd better go."

CHAPTER THREE

The rolling surf hit the white sand at the base of Mount Maunganui. Despite its name, it wasn't a mountain but a conical hill that rose two hundred metres at the point of a narrow peninsular. This was one of New Zealand's top beaches and was crowded with thousands of vacationers. Hundreds of people from toddlers to grandparents crowded the beach and surrounding urban area. Youths in knee length shorts goggled at tanned girls in skimpy attire, while children built sandcastles in the sand. Red and yellow surf patrol flags flew, and two women shared the waves a dozen metres from shore with hundreds of other bathers.

"My God," screeched the younger woman. "That breaker!"

A wave curled up over their heads ready to break. "Dive beneath it," Bree shouted as the wave crashed.

Everything disappeared in a wall of green but the water beneath the surface was calm. Bree rose to the surface, shook wet hair from her eyes and glanced around to find that the wave had broken into a mountain of surf inshore from them. A spluttering Jenny came up beside her. However, behind, another wave was mounting.

"Jump up with it and start swimming," Bree called.

She leaped up in the surge of the next wave began kicking. The crest caught her and she was propelled forward like an express train. After the exhilarating body surf she found the sand scraping her tummy and stood up laughing. Jenny, several metres across from her, also rose and let water slide off her body.

"How did you know what to do?" Jenny shouted above the roar of surf and children's shouts.

"My family took me to Hawaii for a holiday when I was twelve. I reckon I never forgot what to do."

"It shows, too," Jenny replied. "Shall we go and catch another one?"

"Sure," Bree replied and led the race out.

For another forty minutes the pair dived beneath, jumped over, or caught an occasional breaker that carried them ashore. Finally, they staggered out, collapsed onto their beach towels and dried themselves down.

"Well, we did it," Jenny gasped as she ran a finger through her sticky hair.

"What?"

"Had an ocean swim on New Year's Day. With the aeroplane not getting here until noon. I didn't think we would manage it."

"Well, everything was organised. We had out rental car waiting and the motel booked." Bree began to rub sunscreen lotion on her arms. "It's a great little place, too. Far better than those impersonal hotel rooms Colin preferred."

"Bree," Jenny said. "Your promise!"

"Oh, yes." Bree laughed. "I said I wouldn't mention his name."

"Then don't," Jenny replied in a school madam's voice.

They dried in the hot sun and watched the holiday crowd. Music from a radio behind them competed with the shouts of a group of teenagers playing a ball game on the sand and the roar of two boats that zigzagged back and forth beyond the breakers. Jenny rolled over and let the sun warm her back while Bree opened a local woman's magazine she'd bought and began to read.

*

The pair spent the night at a tiny motel that was a complete contrast to the upmarket hotel Bree usually stayed at when she travelled with her husband. It was clean and quiet, though, with comfortable beds, and their rental car was parked right outside the door. Thursday arrived, two days before Bree was due at the conference in Palmerston North, a city five hundred and sixty kilometres southwest across the North Island. According to the map Jenny had studied with enthusiasm, the land between the two centres consisted of mountains and hilly terrain. They'd cross exotic pine forests and Lake Taupo, fly south of three mountains and over forested hill country until they arrived over the Manawatu Plains. They were booked to fly out early on Friday morning on a small link airline.

*

The *West Central Air* hanger at Tauranga airport was an austere building that once belonged to the aero club before they shifted to modern facilities. Inside the untidy interior, a small monoplane had its engine cowling removed, and two men peered at the partially assembled engine.

"Will she be ready, Peter?" one man said. "With our other plane having its annual check, we've no reserve."

"Sure, Vince. I've put the new carburettor in and cleaned the fuel lines out with compressed air. I only have to reassemble it all. Give me an hour and you can take her up for a test flight."

"Okay, see you later." Vince climbed down from the maintenance platform and disappeared outside.

Peter continued to work away for fifteen minutes or so. He whistled to himself and never noticed a visitor until someone coughed. He glanced down and saw a guy in white overalls standing beside the Cessna.

"Gid'day, mate," he said. "Do ya want something?"

The man climbed up the other side of the triangular ladder and flashed an identity badge at Peter. "Jamal Schmidt," he said in an English accent. "I'm from the Cessna head office in The States."

Peter stopped and wiped his hands with a greasy rag. "You don't look like one of those office types to me."

Schmidt laughed. "No, I'm in maintenance, like yourself. I was told you ordered a new carburettor for the Stationair. We've had a bit of trouble with similar models back home. Since I was in the country with the big bosses trying to get a new order from a local crop-dusting firm, they suggested I drop by to see if you had the old carburettor around."

"Sure it's here but it's buggered."

"That's what we're interested in," the Englishman said. "If you don't want it, I'd like to take it home so it can be checked for metal fatigue. We've had several other complaints from operators."

Peter shrugged. "Nah, the casing's okay. We decided it was easier to put a new carburettor in rather than replace all the bits, that's all. It's over on the bench. Take it if you wish."

Schmidt, though, seemed to be in no hurry to leave. He glanced at the work Peter was doing. "Those aren't standard fuel lines are they?" he said.

Peter laughed. "Nope. Everything from your country costs the earth, so we often use locally manufactured stuff or buy it in from Taiwan." He sniffed. "It's just as good and quarter the price."

"Fair enough. Where did you say the old carburettor was?"

Peter turned and pointed.

"Right, I see it," the Englishman said when Peter turned back to face him. "I'll leave you in peace then. Thanks for your help. If there is anything wrong, head office will send your boss an email."

"No problem"' Peter said, shook the man's extended hand and continued joining the fuel lines up.

*

The woman behind the Air New Zealand counter glanced up at the pair from her computer monitor. "We don't handle the West *Central Air* ticketing, Madam," she said to Bree. "Their counter is over beside the rental car kiosks."

"Thank you," Bree said

There seemed to be no reception area for *West Central Air* near the rental car firms.

"There it is," Jenny said, and pointed to a small counter tucked in an alcove. A pile of cardboard boxes almost hid the modest company sign – West Central Air.

"Thank goodness," Bree replied. "We're due to leave in twenty minutes."

A man in a pilot's uniform smiled at them from behind the counter. He glanced at the tickets and banged them with a stamp. "It's only a small six-seat Cessna Stationair," he said after he heard their English accents. "We don't offer the comfort of the Air New Zealand flights." He grinned. "You'll be the only passengers. I'll be glad to have your company." The man laughed when he noticed Jenny's screwed up nose. "My name is Vince Thorton, pilot, attendant and cleaner. We take mail and freight out every morning and fly back again at five in the afternoon. Often, I fly alone. Still want to come?"

"A small aeroplane will be a change, " Bree said. "I've heard it's quite a scenic flight."

The pilot nodded and walked around the counter. "I'll take your luggage. As soon as I get these cartons loaded, we can be off. Be at Departure Gate 3 in about quarter of an hour."

*

The flight was quite unlike any Bree and Jenny had been on before. In an aeroplane the size of a station wagon, and with the wing above them, they had a tremendous view of the country below. It was rugged, steep and covered in thick bush, as Vince called the forest below. Bree sat in the front beside the pilot while Jenny sat in the seat behind.

"We'll be over pine forests soon," Vince said above the murmur of the engine. "Then it's Lake Taupo and the central high country. I'm afraid there's a northerly storm coming in so the mountains may be hidden."

The three volcanoes were visible, though, and still had snow on their shady southern slopes. The wide, twin-peaked Mount Ruapehu towered above the conical shaped Mount Ngauruhoe and smaller Mount Tongariro, while the surrounding land of light brown tussock had a black line cut diagonally across it.

"The Desert Road," Vince said. "Ruapehu, that biggest mountain, is two thousand seven hundred metres high. It's the largest in the North Island."

"Impressive," Jenny replied as she gazed out the window. "Those clouds behind it sure look black, though."

"The storm's coming in quite quickly," Vince replied. "We should be all right, though. We're moving southeast away from it. There's more high country for a while, then you'll see the Manawatu Plains."

The sky behind the three mountains was inky black, and one misty section showed where a downpour covered the landscape.

"Oh my," Bree muttered as the whole northern sky split open in white sheet lightning. Seconds later, thunder rumbled and the Cessna buffeted. Bree grinned at Jenny, who appeared a picture of tranquillity. Her own stomach felt queasy and she concentrated on looking straight ahead through the spinning propeller.

The sky darkened and more sheet lightning cut across the sky in increasing intensity. The Cessna vibrated with each sound. Bree now felt quite ill and reached for the security of a paper bag. Even Jenny had paled a little, but the nonchalant pilot took it in his stride. He reached for his radio, changed frequencies, and a different voice came through the speakers.

"The great divide," he explained. "We're in the central air control district. There's a radar station east of Palmerston North. They're just telling us we're on their scope." He grinned. "Half an hour and we'll be there."

Bree braved a look out a side window where thickly forested hills poked out of misty rain clouds. Visibility dropped and the instruments glowed in semi-darkness. Suddenly, hail hit their aeroplane - pelting stones of ice that drowned the engine noise. It lasted for two minutes or so, and then disappeared as quickly as it came. More lightning flashed but it was behind them, and a ray of sunlight pierced the clouds in the east.

"Almost through," Vince said

Bree caught Jenny's eyes and smiled. She hadn't vomited and her stomach felt as if it could now handle the vibrations. Away ahead, the clouds broke, and green, flat land came into view. This gave her confidence. She glanced at her watch, sighed and brushed a strand of hair out of her eyes. Their arrival time was twenty minutes away. Thank God they were almost there.

*

Possibly one of the loneliest spots in the country on New Year's Eve was Stapleford Hut in the Ruahine Ranges northeast of Palmerston North. This was one of the more remote huts that provided basic shelter for hunters and the more dedicated trampers in the area. As the misty rain turned to a steady downpour and the summer light faded into darkness Ray Barnett walked under the back veranda and removed his drenched rainwear.

If old city acquaintances could see him now they would have commented on the change. His pale skin had become deeply tanned and he'd put on several kilograms of weight over the last two months. His wet hair needed a trim and the old shorts, shirt and solid work boots contrasted to the business suit he'd worn in the city.

"Well, Pattie, we made it before the dark," he said and reached down to stroke the Golden Labrador beside him. The dog shook water off her body and stared at her master with her tail thumping, as Ray continued. "Come on, we'll go inside and get the fire going."

The interior consisted of a kitchen and living area, two bunkrooms and a crude shower that had hot water once the wood waiting in fire box of the ancient metal stove was lit. Ray placed his backpack on the table, found a can of dog food and scooped half the contents into a tin dish for his companion.

"That'll keep you going while I get the fire lit and change into dry clothes," he said.

The dog hesitated and looked up with intelligent eyes. It was as if she didn't want to eat until Ray had something for himself.

Ray ruffled her ears and laughed. "Go ahead. I'll cook myself up something once the fire is going. Perhaps we can warm up some milk for you." He glanced at a calendar on the wall that still had October displayed. That was probably the last time anyone had visited Stapleford Hut.

"Well, this is better than getting ready for one of those New Year office parties," he muttered to himself.

Christmas with Emily and Ken had been depressing. Sure, his in-laws had done everything to make his time enjoyable, almost too much. Emily had fussed around, and the gifts they'd given him were from the heart, especially the photograph album with photos of Maxie's childhood. He appreciated their affection but was glad to leave town and head back to hills in the ex-army Land Rover he'd bought. This was parked a day's trek back at the nearest road head.

So, the lonely man was sound asleep in a narrow bunk with the Golden Labrador on a mattress beside him as the clock ticked past midnight and the rest of the country celebrated the arrival of another new year.

*

The crack sounded like one of those tiny firecrackers. It was muffled but ominous. The engine screamed of tearing metal, spluttered and stopped. The pilot frowned, adjusted some controls and the engine roared to life. However, it howled like a chainsaw gone wrong and cut out again. Everything shuddered and the aeroplane slipped sideways. Dials in front of the pilot competed with a siren and flashing red light for attention.

Jenny gasped and Bree clasped her seat belt and stared at the sky ahead. Vince swore, reached out and pulled a switch. The engine clanged once more, but wouldn't start.

"What is it?" Bree shouted. Her voice reflected the terror in her mind.

"I reckon a piston's seized," Vince replied, his own voice calm. "I'm trying to isolate it.   It could be the fuel line. If we...." There was a clink and a misty vapour poured from the engine "Bugger," Vince swore. "The fuel pipe's broken away. That's aviation fuel pouring out." He pressed the radio transmission button. "Mayday! Mayday! West Central Air Cessna ZK VPB has lost engine power. Our position is...."

Bree stared at Jenny, Vince's voice fading to the background. The windshield was splattered with oil and the distinct smell of aviation fuel entered the cockpit. Below, thick hills of forest poked out of the misty clouds. It appeared as if they were suspended in the air and the trees were rushing towards them.

"Can you talk to the air control," Vince shouted at Bree. "I need to bring the nose up."

Bree nodded, clamped the spare headphones on and spoke. "This is the Cessna. I'm a passenger. Vince is trying to pull the nose up."

"Central Air Control. Cessna ZK VPB. Can we have more details, please?"

Bree swallowed and pressed the red transmit button. In a voice far calmer than she felt she described what happened.

"And your name, Madam?" the voice cut in.

"Bree Ashworth."

"Good, Bree," the voice said. "Has Vince started the motor?"

"No," Bree replied. "The windshield is covered in oil."

"Has Vince pulled the nose up?" The controller's calm voice continued.

Bree glanced up "Yes. Our nose is up but the propeller has almost stopped turning. We appear to be level." She described everything, while the pilot wrestled with the controls and the Cessna's wings straightened.

Seconds that seemed like eternity passed before Vince touched her arm and smiled in appreciation. "I've stopped the dive and can talk on the radio now," he said and immediately began to read out technical data of their position, rate of descent and weather conditions. "We have five minutes at the most," he reported. "...Steep terrain all around. I'm heading into a valley. There's fog below and the ground view is obstructed..."

Bree glanced back at Jenny's pale face. "We'll make it," she whispered.

Jenny nodded and attempted a smile. "We swam on New Year's Day, Bree." Her voice was soft.

"Yes, we did. And we'll go back for more before we leave to go home..."

Jenny grimaced and pulled her seat belt tighter.

Beside them, clouds blurred past. Rain mixed with the fuel on the windscreen to make lines of smudged rainbow colours.

"Hang on!' Vince said in an emotionless voice. "We're going in."

CHAPTER FOUR

Dawn arrived early. It wasn't cold, but misty rain clung to the forest around Stapleford Hut. Ray glanced at the nearby hills and decided to leave his departure until the weather improved. His destination was another hut five hours away over a saddle, through a narrow valley and up to the top end of the forest where tussock took over. From there he would take linear studies at five hundred metre drops in altitude to see how several noxious plants had spread since a similar study had been taken five years earlier. Preliminary research had shown that the unwanted plants had made significant gains at the lower levels but at these higher altitudes the native secondary growth managed to outgrow the exotic intruders.

Ray washed his small bundle of dirty laundry, cleaned out the stove firebox and set it up ready for instant lighting by the next visitor. He grinned. It would probably be himself in about ten days on his way back. He swept the hut out and walked outside to study the conditions again. The rain had stopped but grey clouds still clung to the high ridges. It was almost eleven so he either had to start soon or wait another day.

"Shall we go, Pattie?" he asked his dog, "or would you like another lazy day?"

Pattie wagged her tail and looked up at Ray. Her tail beat and she trotted along the path a few metres, stopped and barked.

"Okay," Ray said with a laugh. "We'll go. I need to finish packing though. Won't be long."

Three hours later, he regretted his decision. The clouds had dropped and the pair found themselves walking through dense fog. The so-called track was overgrown and it was only the shiny pieces of metal nailed to trees at regular intervals that showed the way. Several of these had become obscured by undergrowth or lost over the years and, on one occasion, it was only with Pattie's help that Ray found his way back to his last marker to discover he'd gone the wrong way.

They stopped mid-afternoon and had a cold meal of sandwiches or dog food, depending on their tastes, and continued their journey.

An hour later, Pattie stopped and barked.

"What is it, girl?" Ray asked.

Pattie's ears were on full alert and she stared skyward.

Ray heard the object of his dog's attention. High above them an aircraft engine spluttered, roared to life and died. Ray grimaced and strained to hear more. Something was there, the sort of whistling sound of an object moving.

"Hush, girl," Ray said when Pattie gave a yelp and turned her head.

Ray also turned and gasped. An aeroplane appeared out of the clouds across from them. It was in trouble, too. No engine roared, but the whistling air was accompanied by the twang of metal hitting something.

As he watched, spellbound, the aircraft glided on and disappeared into another cloudbank. For several seconds Ray heard nothing. He waited but still jumped in fright when an almighty crash thundered through the trees.

"Come on, Pattie," he said. "Find it, girl. If anyone survives that they'll need our help."

Pattie barked in reply and headed off the track down a steep slope to the stream two hundred metres below. They were halfway down when the aircraft exploded and a fireball filled the valley ahead.

"We're too late, girl," Ray whispered. "Nobody could survive that."

Pattie, though, disappeared through the undergrowth.

"Pattie!" Ray yelled. "Wait for me." He had never seen his pet so determined.

*

"Bree!" screamed a voice a million miles away. "Bree! Wake up! It's me, Jenny. My God, please wake up."

Bree opened her eyes and gasped for breath as a cold hand touched her face. She spluttered, managed to clear her throat and looked at Jenny. The young woman's face was all eyes, hair and blood. Further inspection showed the blood was pouring from a gash across Jenny 's forehead.

"Oh, Bree," Jenny cried. "You're okay?"

"I guess," Bree replied and attempted to sit up. She realized her legs were in water and there was nothing beside her. The wing and fuselage were gone. Crunched up metal was pushed back almost to her chest and pieces of glue-type glass particles were everywhere.

But the plane had stopped moving and the only noise that accompanied Jenny's voice was a gurgling stream. Everything stunk of aviation fuel. It would take only a spark!

Bree slammed her hand against her seatbelt control and almost fell into the water as the device released. "We have to get away," she shouted. "The plane might blow up."

How they did it, she couldn't remember, but she and Jenny managed to drag themselves upstream from the Cessna. The foliage on both banks was too dense to even consider going ashore. The knee-deep water swirled around and splashed Bree's thighs, the coldness helping to restore normality to her numbed mind. A horrible thought made her shudder. "The pilot," she cried. "Where's the pilot?"

"He saved us, Bree," Jenny panted. "There was this massive rock that he steered into...." Her chin trembled. "The whole of his side of the aeroplane just crunched up like a flattened soda can. He never had a chance."

"He's dead?"

Jenny nodded. "I thought you were, too. I ended up in the stream and saw Vince first." She shuddered. "You don't want to look. It's not him any more."

They stumbled on, holding to each other for support in the current.

"There's a gravel ledge ahead," Bree gasped when they arrived at a bend. "Make for it."

As they did so, the Cessna exploded with a thunder-like crack. A fireball of gasoline filled the area they'd just evacuated, shooting debris and putrid black smoke into the air. A scorching wind flung the two women into the water. By the time Bree crawled to the surface, the fireball had gone, and smoke poured skyward in billowing clouds.

Bree turned to find she was still gripping Jenny's arm. "Thanks," she whispered. "If it wasn't for you, I would have been in the middle of that."

Jenny nodded. "Makes us about even, doesn't it?" she replied in a solemn voice.

"Suppose it does," Bree said, then managed a shaky smile. "My God, what a couple of drenched rats we are."

"But alive rats," Jenny replied. She staggered forward to the gravel ledge, sat down, and wrapped her arms about her knees. She stared around with uncertainty in her eyes. "What now?"

"We stay here," Bree replied. "Vince gave our position. I'm sure there will be a search made."

"In this mist and rain?"

"Okay," Bree admitted. "We could be here the night." She shivered. "It's cold. We must be quite high above sea level."

Now that they were out of immediate danger her thoughts turned to her aching ribs. She probed her side, then gasped when her fingers pushed on a tender spot.

"We'll need to get up the bank," Jenny said. "It's thick with willows, but there are larger trees further in. There should be space beneath them." She stood up and placed an arm around Bree's shoulders. "You're shivering and look as white as a ghost."

"Aftershock," Bree whispered. "I'll be okay." She wasn't though. Her head felt light, and Jenny's concerned face went out of focus. She gritted her teeth and concentrated on moving up the small bank. Sharp grass cut into her arms and the willows were so close together she could barely squeeze between them.

Jenny held branches back and helped her up a slippery section.

"Thanks." Bree squinted her eyes in pain, then sank to her knees. Crawling, she made better progress and soon she and Jenny were through the band of willows. Ahead, tall trees towered above fern, grass, creeper and long, black vines. Everything dripped water but it didn't matter. She and Jenny were saturated anyhow.

"The vegetation is different than at home," Jenny panted as she flattened a clump of fern with a foot.

"I read that they have no dangerous native animals or snakes," Bree replied. She held her stomach and tried to keep her head clear. It felt as though the blood had stopped flowing.

For several more moments, they continued climbing until the undergrowth cleared and they found themselves under a canopy of gigantic trees. Apart from occasional drips they were also out of the rain.

"This'll do," Jenny said. "I'd hate to get lost in here." She guided Bree in beside tree roots thicker than her arm and knelt beside her. "Now, let's look at your wound."

*

"I found something to help," Jenny said. She walked around the tree where Bree lay clutching her stomach. "How is it?"

"Stopped bleeding, I think." Bree's smile turned to a grimace when she attempted to manipulate her body.

"Everything's gone," Jenny said. "Even my bum bag that had my passport and money."

Bree sighed. "I've lost my things, too, but documents can be replaced. I have a copy of everything stored on my website."

"Good thinking," Jenny said and turned her attention back to their more immediate concerns. She held up a piece of blue material. "There are bits of metal strewn everywhere. This old shirt is the only thing of any use I could find." She shrugged. "It's wet but I thought if you pressed it against your wound it might help." She plunked herself down and wiped a hand across her brow. "Stupid idea, wasn't it?'

"No, it'll be a great help," Bree replied. "Thanks."

"I reckon we're here for the night," Jenny said. "The rain's heavier. The explosion blew itself out so there's not even smoke now. An aeroplane could fly thirty feet above us and not see a thing..."

CHAPTER FIVE

The hours slipped by without any break in the weather. Bree had fallen asleep and Jenny had no idea when darkness would arrive. It was after eight so there wouldn't be too much daylight left. Her clothes had dried but everything clung like shrunken cardboard, and she could do with a sweater. She felt the old shirt that had been draped over a branch. It was almost dry and she tucked it around Bree, then stood up and stretched.

Without Bree to talk to she felt nervous in this strange forest. It was so quiet! Sure, the rain could be heard sweeping the bushes, the water in the rising stream roared, and a few unknown birds called in the distance - but that was it. The smell of damp moisture now superseded the stench of lingering smoke from the aeroplane explosion. She considered returning to the crash site but the thought of seeing the dead pilot sent shivers up her spine. The one earlier view, of the friendly man reduced to a pile of mangled flesh squashed between tortured metal, was enough. Thank God Bree was with her.

She sat down again and rested her head against the tree trunk. Not far away, two little birds darted from branch to branch with their tails spread out like a fan. They must be the fantails she'd read about in the tourist literature on the flight across the Pacific. They seemed almost tame as they fluttered around just out of reach.

The grunting noise off to her left made her jump. She got slowly to her feet and crept around the base of the tree. Something was there, and it was big! Bree said there were no native animals in New Zealand but if this wasn't an animal, what was it? She stole another glance around. Only a few yards away stood a hog, a huge one with tusks and a mean expression.

Jenny clung onto the tree trunk and gulped in sheer terror. Caution overcame fear and she decided to remain still. The pig sort of blinked, if that is what pigs do, grunted, turned and disappeared through the foliage. Jenny heaved a sigh of relief and glanced up. The fantails were back. Their friendly nature helped to slow down her racing heart.

As it grew dark, the branches around became sinister looking arms. Only the trunk gave a sense of security. Jenny was cold, itchy, and her limbs were cramped, but she was not about to leave the tree. Darkness encroached even further and the only visible object was a brief glimpse of silver water tumbling below. In the night air it seemed closer. Perhaps it was. Jenny pulled her knees up and wrapped her arms around them. She shivered. Another eight hours of this! My God, it would be one of the longest nights in her life.

"Okay," she muttered as her empty stomach rumbled. "I needed to go on a diet anyway."

Her thoughts drifted back to Sunset Grove primary. Christine, her friend from way back in secondary school days had laughed when she said she applied for a position there. All the schools in the better boroughs of London were highly sort after. Jenny had only put in a cheeky application at Sunset Grove, when she had applied at a half dozen for schools south of the Thames River. She chuckled to herself. Those schools turned her down and she'd all but given up on Sunset Grove when she'd received a call and was asked in for an interview. But that was history. She won the position and loved the job, until that bastard attacked her. God, that scared hell out of her.

"You're deep in thought, Jenny."

Jenny swung around and saw Bree's eyes, white in the darkness. "My God, don't scare me like that!" she hissed.

"Sorry," Bree replied. "I shouldn't have wakened you."

"I wasn't asleep," Jenny replied.

"So, you snore when you're awake, do you?"

Jenny laughed. "I guess I must have been. Anyhow, it's good to have someone to talk with."

"Yeah, the place gets to you a bit, doesn't it?"

"You said there were no animals here. You were damn wrong, you know."

"I was?"

"There was a whopping great hog that ambled through when you were asleep," Jenny said.

"Hog?"

"Yeah. Massive brute with tusks like an elephant and beady little eyes."

Bree studied Jenny. "You're serious, aren't you?"

"Of course. Why would I make up a story like that?"

"Sure it was a hog?"

Jenny nodded.

"But hogs don't climb trees."

"Of course not. Don't be silly."

"Then what's that looking at us?" Bree whispered and glanced up above them.

Jenny followed her friend's gaze and gasped. Two red eyes glared down at her, unblinking, from the very tree they were under. There was not a sound. "Damn," she gasped. "What is it?"

"I've no idea," Bree replied. "But I reckon it's as scared of us as we are of it."

"A cougar," Jenny spluttered. Her confidence struck a new low.

"They don't have wild cats in New Zealand. I know that much."

Far off something hooted, and Jenny swung around. "God, what's that?"

"An owl," Bree replied. "They have them. They're called Moreporks. That's what they sound like."

Jenny listened. It did sound like 'more pork'. Like the fantails that afternoon, the bird cry made her feel a little better. "Red eyes has gone," she said after a quick glance back at the branches towering above them.

"I'm glad the rain's stopped and the moon's come out," Bree said.

"True, but the stream's up."

The pair continued chatting, while around them, the New Zealand bush life continued as it had done for hundreds of years. Jenny heard the opossum on the branch above them move away on its nocturnal search for food, while overhead, more clouds gathered as the northerly storm swept in off the Tasman Sea.

*

Jenny awoke, stiff and cold to find the darkness was replaced by an eerie fog, so thick that trees only a few feet away appeared as shimmering shadows. She stood and noticed two more things. The water was closer; in fact she could see it lapping branches at the edge of the fog. Secondly, she realized she was alone.

Adrenaline gripped her stomach. "Bree!" she screamed. "Where are you?"

"Coming." Bree's voice came from further up the bank and a moment later she appeared out of the mist. "Call of nature," she added. "You were sound asleep. Can you come here a moment?"

"Damn," Jenny replied but walked towards Bree. "What a night. I reckon I woke up twenty times and every bone in my body complained. God, I'm filthy." She laughed when she reached Bree.

"What?" Bree ran a hand over mud-stained blouse and flicked hair from her eyes. Mud covered her shoes, legs and arms.

"If Patricia could see us now."

Miss Patricia McCarthy was the somewhat prim and proper Deputy Headteacher at their school. She was older than Bree and had been on the school staff for fifteen years. Nobody had ever seen her in casual clothes, and the gossip was that she lived and breathed school twenty-four hours a day.

Bree laughed. "She does take life seriously..."

"So, what do you want?" Jenny added.

"Have you noticed the stream?"

"It's more like a river now. Why?"

"I went back to the crash site. I thought I might find something useful but..."

"Go on."

"The wreck's gone."

Bree led Jenny along a narrow animal track that twisted along the bank. Five minutes later, they arrived at a small clearing that overlooked the raging torrent. Jenny gasped. Even in the fog the power of the brown swirling water could be seen. Frothy waves carried debris by. One branch swept past, caught the undergrowth on the bank and was sucked under. One end lurched up, water splashed around in a whirlpool, wrenched it away, and the whole thing disappeared in the whiteness ahead.

"I'm glad we never landed when it was like that," Jenny shouted above the roar of water.

Bree pointed out across the water. "This is where we crashed. You can see the broken branches on the other side."

Jenny peered out and nodded. "That's the rock Vince hit," she said. "Half the aeroplane was wrapped around his body."

"But the wreckage is gone," Bree said.

"It's probably under the water."

"But more likely its been swept away." Bree grabbed Jenny's arm. "Do you hear that booming?"

Jenny listened. Above the roar of water there was a crunching rumble. "Yes. What is it?"

"I read once that flood waters can even roll boulders over."

"Okay," Jenny said with a shrug.

Bree sounded almost exasperated. "Look up, Jenny. What do you see?"

"The fog and trees overhanging the stream."

"Exactly. When the fog lifts and rescue aircraft come, how will they know we're here? There are snapped off branches and logs everywhere. Even if they see the aeroplane it could be miles downstream."

Jenny's eyes opened wide. "So, just waiting here for a helicopter to fly in and haul us out won't happen?" She bit on her bottom lip. "So what can we do?"

"Go downstream as far as we can. If we stay near to the stream we won't get lost and we'll also be able to see any aircraft that come searching."

Jenny stared at the flooded stream. For a moment, despair filtered through her mind. They had no warm clothes, no food and nothing to signal a rescue plane, even if it came.

"So, we're on our own?" she whispered.

Bree shook her head. "No, I don't think so, but it could be days before a search party finds us. Vince sent our position just before we crashed so they'll know the area we're in. As long as we don't do anything silly, someone will find us, I'm sure of that."

"Just like school," Jenny replied.

Bree frowned.

"Well, no matter how bad anything is, you manage to instil confidence in the staff. Remember that parent who was going to sue the school for neglect and God knows what else? Old Patricia was bursting an ulcer and you called his bluff."

"Yes. He was a pompous little man who tried to blame the school for his child's misbehaviour. I just pointed that out to him."

"So, you think we've still got a chance?"

"Sure," Bree replied. "We won't die of thirst. That's something, isn't it?"

Jenny had to smile. Now, if only the damn fog would lift.

*

Three hours later, after pushing through thick ground cover, jumping across rocks beside raging waters and slithering through razor sharp grass, Bree called a halt.

"Jenny, I need to stop," she puffed.

Jenny turned. In spite of the drizzle that soaked them whenever they left the trees, most of the moisture on her face was perspiration. A smudge of mud covered it and her arms showed a rash of cuts from the grass. "Are you okay?" she asked when she noticed Bree's face white face and blue lips.

Bree grimaced. "I've a pain across my ribs."

"Well, why didn't you say so earlier? Wherever we're going, a few extra minutes won't matter."

Bree leaned against an available tree trunk and ran a hand down her neck. "It's okay. I think I bumped it when we climbed over those last logs."

"Sit down and I'll look."

The old shirt had been ripped into a bandage and wrapped around her middle. Now, though, it was dirty and black with congealed blood.

Bree's arms were also scratched and an ugly bruise had appeared on one leg. "I think it's just the lack of food but I feel quite ill," she admitted.

"Yeah, I know," Jenny replied. "I'm thirsty, too, but don't want to risk drinking that filthy stream water."

The pair searched around until they found a shallow dip that was dry and sheltered from a wind that had risen. Jenny unwrapped the bandage and examined Bree's wound. She gently pulled away the last piece of material, then frowned.

"How long has it been bleeding?" she asked in her sternest school ma'am voice.

"I never noticed..."

"Bree," Jenny cut in. "It looks like it's been bleeding all morning. You're just about dead on your feet. My God, I'm exhausted and I haven't that whopping great cut. We're going nowhere until you feel better. I'll rewrap the wound."

"With that bandage?"

"No," Jenny replied. She took off her blouse, ripped a five-inch strip off the bottom and put it on again. "All the teenagers wear tops that expose their tummies," she said with a laugh. "It's not clean but it's better than the old one." She walked a few feet down to the stream, dipped the old shirt in and returned. With the wet rag, she gently cleaned the wound and rebound it with the second makeshift bandage.

"There that's better," she said. "Hopefully, the pressure will stop the bleeding."

"Thanks," Bree replied. She wiped her eyes, leaned back and took her shoes and socks off. "Thought so," she whispered.

"Damn," Jenny responded.

Both Bree's feet were swollen. The underside of her right foot had a massive blister stretching from big toe to little.

Jenny opened her mouth but stopped when she saw her companion's face. Instead, she placed an arm around Bree's shoulders and gave her an affectionate squeeze, then sat down and removed her own footwear. Her own feet were red and wrinkly but there was no broken skin.

"So, we stay here," she said.

Ten minutes later, they heard an engine roar, and a small aeroplane flew out of the clouds. Jenny jumped up and ran, screaming out onto rocks by the stream. She waved and jumped; almost fell in the water in the process but the aircraft continued on downstream. There was no indication that she had been seen.

"Damn," she snorted. "I was too slow. They had gone before I got into the open. I don't know why I wasted my time screaming, either."

"You never know," Bree replied. "Someone may have heard you."

*

Bree's words were close to the truth. In the dense bush behind them, Ray had also seen the aeroplane fly up the valley. As the engine noise retreated, a distant girl's scream sounded faintly above the stream's roar.

Pattie barked and looked at her master with her tail thumping.

"Okay, Pattie," Ray said. "Go find her. But don't go too fast. Okay?"

Pattie woofed, gave Ray an understanding glance and disappeared through the undergrowth.

Ray smiled. They set a frantic pace and he hoped Pattie would catch up to them up before they became too lost.

"Someone wearing shoes like that could only be business women," he murmured, his worry increasing. This was rugged terrain. Especially for someone unseasoned to it. He shook his head. "I'd have thought the pilot, at least, would have had enough sense to stay put."

He took his map from a jacket pocket and glanced along to his estimated position. The stream wound on for about a kilometre before the water was dumped over a hundred and twenty metre waterfall. The valley he was in had a dead end. The only way out was back the way he'd come.

*

Jenny felt apprehensive. Bree had dozed off and the loneliness of this strange forest gripped her again. Earlier optimism disappeared when no other aeroplanes appeared, and the drizzle turned to a sweeping rain that even dripped into their shelter. She sat huddled up and stared at the steam. The water sounded louder. Perhaps there were rapids ahead.

God, she was hungry!

A sound in the bushes ahead made her heart race. Damn, it could be another hog! She was about to shake Bree awake but instead chastised herself for cowardliness and stood up. With one hand brushing the tree trunk for security, she edged her way around it and stared though the undergrowth. There wasn't a lot to see in the dim light; tree trunks spaced haphazardly around, ferns hugging the ground, and those black vines dangling everywhere.

For someone used to urban streets, buildings, traffic and people, the scene was as surreal as a fantasy movie. She closed her eyes. Perhaps when she opened them again, she'd find her class of children waiting for her to read them another story. That was always a popular time. Every afternoon she would gather the children around and read them a story from one of the oversized picture books in the classroom library.

Jenny's eyes snapped open and her mind rushed back to the present. Something was coming! "Bree," she whispered. "Bree! Wake up!"

Bree jerked awake, looked disorientated for a second, and frowned. The fern ahead was shaking as something moved beneath it.

Both women were silent, watching, until Jenny saw a flash of ginger fur. She gave a stifled gasp. This turned to relief when the animal struggled out from the undergrowth and rose to its feet.

"A dog," Bree said.

The Golden Labrador ran towards them, stopped and sat down. Its manner was friendly.

"Hello, young fellow," she said. "Where did you come from?"

The dog came forward with its tail wagging.

Jenny laughed. "It's someone's pet," she said with relief in her voice. She knelt down and patted the newcomer. "Hello, girl," she said. "I'm Jenny and this is Bree. We're lost."

The dog glanced at them both, then sat with her tongue out and lips curled up in almost a smile. Though wet and mud-splattered, she looked healthy and wore a collar. Jenny reached for it and read the label. As well as a registration number it had a name stamped on the green tag.

"So, you're Pattie," Bree said. "Hi, Pattie."

The dog's response was immediate. She stared at Bree with her tail thumping and held out a paw, which Bree shook.

Jenny patted the newcomer and laughed. "Where's your master, Pattie?" she asked.

Pattie barked, ran a few metres, sat down and turned to face them. Her tail stopped wagging.

Jenny frowned and called Pattie back. However, the dog only padded half a dozen steps towards her before she stopped and whined softly.

"What is it girl?" Jenny asked.

She walked forward to Patty but just as she reached out, Pattie yelped and retreated back several metres. She stopped, sat down and waited.

"Silly dog," Jenny muttered and stepped forward again. Again, though, the dog moved further away but remained in sight.

"Perhaps she wants us to follow," Bree said.

"But that's back upstream."

"So? A dog in this condition wouldn't be way out here by herself. I reckon she's better fed than we are."

"You're right," Jenny replied. "So, what are you waiting for?"

Aches and pains were forgotten as the two crash victims followed the Golden Labrador up the hillside. Pattie rushed ahead but always stayed in view. If the women were slow, she'd rush back, or sit until they reached her, before running ahead again.

A quarter of an hour later, Pattie gave a quiet yelp and, for the first time, bounded away out of sight. Bree looked at Jenny and smiled. "She'll be back," she said. "Let's rest a minute."

Two minutes later, Pattie reappeared, wagged her tail as if reassured they were still there and disappeared again. A moment later, a male voice vibrated through the undergrowth. "Okay, Pattie," he said. "I know! I know! Patience girl, I take up more room than you."

The undergrowth parted and a man appeared. His tanned face broke into a smile when he saw the pair staring at them. "Well, g'day," he said in the broad New Zealand accent the pair were still getting used to. "I guess you two ladies are from the plane that came down yesterday." He held out a hand as his eyes settled on Bree. "Ray Barnett's my name. You were bloody hard to catch up with, you know."

Jenny's initial feeling of delight turned to a quivering feeling that surged through her body. Her mind flashed back to her classroom at Sunset Grove in London and the attack.

"Bree," she whispered and clutched her friend's arm.

"I think it'll be okay," Bree replied but Jenny noticed there was a quiver in her friend's voice, as well.

CHAPTER SIX

Sergeant Hugh Trendle wiped rain from his eyes and pulled the zipper of his parka higher. It wasn't any good, though. Already the water from the downpour had run inside, and his shirt was saturated. Oh, well, his bottom half was wet. He used the guide rope to steady himself, and fastened a steel cable hook to the crushed aeroplane wing mounting.

"Okay!" he said in the mobile radio pinned to his collar. "Just give me a moment to get out of the way."

His companion grabbed him and hauled him ashore out of the thigh deep current. He nodded a thank you and waved at the helicopter above. For a moment nothing happened. The helicopter appeared to waver as the cable tightened. There was a scream of metal, and the wing of the aircraft wreckage lifted into the air away from the fuselage.

"That'll do," Hugh shouted in the radio. "There's someone there all right." He turned to his companion. "What do you see, Eric?"

"It's the pilot, I'd say. Poor bugger never had a chance." Constable Eric Meech grabbed the safety rope and plodded forward in the current. He peered beyond the mangled corpse and moved a flapping sheet of metal aside. "There's nobody else here, Hugh," he called back.

For several moments both men methodically searched the wreckage before they made their way back to the shore. "What do you think, Eric?" Hugh said.

"Only half the fuselage is here, Sarge. I think it hit the cliff, split down the middle and was carried here in the flood."

"Over the falls?"

Eric rubbed a hand over his wet stubble. "I'm not sure," he said. "The fall's two kilometres upstream from here and, if all the weather and flood reports fit in, the stream wasn't in flood when the Cessna came down." He nodded at the bank where flattened grass and mud showed where the floodwaters had dropped. "But mountain streams rise and fall pretty quickly in these storms."

"So, what's your theory?" Though Hugh Trendle was the senior officer, in these situations, Eric Meech the bush country expert.

"There's not a lot to go on but I'd say the pilot flew over the falls."

"Why?"

"You can't see it because of the flood but under normal conditions this stream is littered with boulders. The only deep spot is a sort of lake that forms at the bottom of the waterfall. I reckon he tried to land there in deeper water rather than hit the trees or boulders."

"So what happened?"

"Wind currents are unpredictable in this narrow valley. My guess is the wind caught the plane, as he was about to come in and flipped it sideways into the far cliff. Once the flood waters drop we can search for signs of the collision."

"And the passengers?"

"They'll either be in the missing half of the fuselage or be downstream somewhere. With this water speed they could be carried half way to the coast."

"But they're dead?"

Eric nodded. "By the look of this wreckage, I doubt if they survived the initial strike. It's strange though."

"You mean that last radio message?"

"Yes, it happened so quickly. It sounded like more than an engine failure."

"I know, but we'll leave that to the Inspector of Air Accidents to piece together. Let's get back up to the chopper. I'll ask the pilot to do a quick search above the falls before we head home. Another crew will come in and get the body."

Eric nodded. "Go downstream, Sarge," he suggested. "We may find more of the wreckage. This bit wouldn't have come over the falls, that I'm certain."

"Okay," Hugh replied. "If we're only looking for bodies, time's not important, is it?"

"I could be wrong," Eric replied.

"But probably aren't. Anyhow, it'll be dark in an hour. We'll get another search organised at first light. The ground search has been called off for now, too. They were in the wrong valley anyhow."

He waved at the helicopter and it moved in to hover above them. In twenty minutes they'd be back at Palmerston North Airport with another hard day's work completed. Air crashes were different from the usual road accidents Hugh attended, but the result was much the same. There were still reports to write and grieving relations to talk to. Oh, yes, the United Kingdom High Commissioner's Office would have to be contacted, as well. As the two policemen were lifted into the helicopter, a second craft flew over. The name of a national television network was emblazoned across its fuselage.

"Damn," Hugh muttered. "An accident like this will do hell to the tourist industry."

Ray hadn't really formed a mental image of the women he was looking for but the sight of the two made him smile. It was that look of utter relief in their eyes that caught his attention. Both were dressed in street clothes, and the younger woman had a blue blouse that was ripped away allowing a white tummy to show. The women's arms were scratched; a few bruises showed and their legs were mud- splattered. Unlike most girls at this time of the year, they were not tanned. Blue lips and white fingers accentuated their pale skin colour.

"Hi, Ray," one of the women said. "My name's Bree." She smiled and gripped Ray's hand. "This is my friend, Jenny."

Ray grinned. "English?" he asked.

"We are. Our accent is noticeable, I guess."

"G'day, Jenny, Bree," Ray said and smiled at their nervousness.

For a second there was a pause in the trio's conversation.

"I love your dog," Bree finally said.

Ray turned to Pattie. "Yeah, she's a good one." He rubbed the dog's head. "You found them, girl," he said. "That's grand."

Pattie's tail wagged and she looked pleased with the compliment. Ray turned back to the women. "We'll get you both something to eat and perhaps a warm jersey to wear." He slid a massive backpack off his shoulders and lifted two khaki jerseys out.

"They're be a bit big, but put them on. You both look cold. I'll see what else I've got." He grinned. "One doesn't usually meet young women this far out. Usually it's hunters, who have a week's growth on their chin, and you have to stay upwind from them."

Bree smiled. "We're pretty filthy, too," she said. She accepted the jersey handed to her and pulled it on, pulling the overlong sleeves up, before turning to Jenny who was also wriggling into the second garment. "This would really thrill Patricia, wouldn't it?"

"Sure would," Jenny said. They both laughed and shared the joke with Ray.

"A toffee-nosed boss," he said. "I know the sort."

"She's not," Jenny replied. "Bree's the boss, Patricia's the deputy headteacher at the school where we work." She screwed her nose up. "Patricia's my boss, though."

Ray grinned. The word headteacher sounded so quaint. It hadn't been used in New Zealand for as long as he could remember. His first impression of these two English women was favourable, though. Bree was the quieter one but seemed to ooze confidence. It didn't surprise him to find out she was a school principal.

He coughed and reddened a little when he caught Bree's eyes on him. It was as if she could read his mind. "I've a first aid kit here," he hastily added. "What say we clean that nasty wound up then I'll pop the billy on, warm us some hot coffee and have a spot to eat."

The 'billy' was an old aluminium saucepan that Ray filled with fresh water from a bottle. He sat a small gas cooker on the ground and soon tiny blue flames were heating the water. "Or would you rather have soup?" he said. "I've got a packet here somewhere. I made some sandwiches earlier. Marmite and lettuce."

"Coffee and sandwiches sound wonderful," Bree said. "But can we help?"

"I'll erect the tent later. You can give me a hand." Ray smiled, pulled a mobile phone from his pocket and nodded at the red pulsing light. "We're here for the night, I'm afraid. We're out of range. Perhaps it'll work from one of the top peaks tomorrow."

*

The ointment and bandage Ray produced were of high quality and Bree was impressed by the way he removed the old shirt bandage and tended to the wound. He frowned at the sight of swollen flesh and clotted blood but she made no comment as he dabbed it with warm water, applied liberal quantities of ointment from a tube and re-bandaged everything.

"So, why are you here, Ray?" she said after he had finished. "You aren't a hunter nor do you spend your life outdoors all the time."

Ray laughed. "Observant of you, Bree," he replied. "How did you work that all out?"

"You've no rifle, at least there's none in sight. You're tanned but look more like a professional person..." She flushed and turned her eyes away. "I'm sorry. It's none of my business."

"That's fine," Ray said. "I'm a botanist doing a government contract. We have trouble with the spread of exotic animals and plants in our native forests. Goats, for example, eat all the undergrowth, and exotic plants, rather than native plants, become the secondary growth. Some species have all but wiped out much of our fern life." He shrugged. "That's the bit I'm concerned about. I'm collecting data on the spread of unwanted plants and seeing how the native species cope."

"And do they?" Jenny cut in.

"It's not too bad up here. We've had a huge cull of goats and deer over the last few years so the native species are getting re-established. At lower levels, though, it's a different story." He chatted on for several moments as he distributed the sandwiches and poured boiling water into two tin mugs. "Excuse the china," he said as he handed one to Bree. "I've some jars of sugar and powdered milk around somewhere. Help yourselves."

Bree raised her eyebrows in surprise, but found two jars and a teaspoon. The hot coffee and food was therapeutic and her hands warmed on the hot mug.

"You stay there," Jenny said when she rose to help Ray unroll an orange and blue tent.

Bree offered only a slight protest. She leaned back and watched the man clip aluminium poles together and loop-on anchor ropes. A few moments later the structure was erected. Ray zipped back the front flap and Pattie ran inside.

"She knows where to get out of the cold," he said with a chuckle. "I reckon she could just about assemble the tent herself if she had to. Go on in. The wind's quite cold."

Bree crawled in and sat on the blue synthetic floor. The interior was amazingly large and comfortable. She squeezed back, patted Pattie and watched as Jenny crawled in beside her.

"You look exhausted, Bree," Jenny said.

"It's a reaction, I guess. Now we're safe I realize how tired I really am."

"Then lie down," Jenny said. "I can help Ray. " She grinned. "If he needs any help, that is."

Bree smiled. Their desperate situation had turned into something relaxing and almost comfortable. She lay back, her eyes heavy. A moment later, she slipped asleep with one arm around the Labrador beside her.

*

Bree woke with a cutting pain across her body; her left shoulder was stiff, and one leg felt as though it was disjointed at the knee. She shifted it, hit someone and realized where she was. Pattie was gone and Jenny lay beside her.

A sound of the flap moving made her twist her head. God, that small effort made her shoulder feel worse.

"I brought you a cuppa coffee." The unfamiliar New Zealand accent filled the darkness. "Your wound hurts, doesn't it?"

Bree ignored her aching shoulder and sat up. Ray was silhouetted against a rectangle of stars. "Thanks," she said and reached for the steaming mug. "How did you know I was awake?"

"A guess," Ray said. "You've been restless for quite some time. Maxie used to say..." He stopped and glanced away. "It doesn't matter."

"No, I'm interested," Bree replied. "I find this time of the night is so lonely at times. Things seem to build up out of proportion. If you're feeling ill it seems twice as bad." She smiled and sipped the coffee. "So, tell me about Maxie. Is she your wife?"

Ray squatted down under the flap that he'd pinned back. "Was," he said softly. "She died a few months back."

"Oh, I'm sorry," Bree said.

"On lonely nights I think of her," he continued. "Often I've had a dream and wake up with her words on my mind. It's always as she was... a laughing student." He glanced at Jenny. "She was a little like your friend here. You know, easy to smile... "

Bree smiled. Somehow she sensed he needed to talk, and she let him as she nursed her hot coffee.

"It goes back to before I met her," Ray said. "She had a congenital heart problem and, as a teenager, had a couple of operations. When I met her at university she was so normal, then one day I saw this massive scar across her tummy." He smiled softly. "She laughed about it and said it cured her from wearing bikinis. Anyhow, for over five years she was fine, then, without a warning, she had this massive heart attack. She pulled through, but was never the same." He turned away and wiped his eyes.

"I've never told a soul before. I've no family. Maxie's parents have been very supportive but are affected as much as I am." He sipped his coffee. "Anyway, she had this emergency operation. That was it, really. She never came out of the anaesthetic."

"Oh my."

"It was a gamble. Her life expectancy was numbered in weeks, anyhow. She loved life too much to slowly fade away. The operation would have given her a better quality of life those last few months, but probably wouldn't have extended it." He shrugged. "It was a long shot that failed."

"So you came out here to get away from everything that reminded you of her?"

"I guess," Ray replied.

"And does being alone with Pattie help?"

"No," Ray admitted. "I think having Pattie has helped but on nights like this my mind goes back. God, I'm getting melancholy aren't I?"

"So?" Bree said. "You have every right to be." She smiled, changing the subject. "Is it my imagination or is it warmer tonight?"

"I think the storm's moved on. At this time of the year it can get sweltering up here in these valleys." His eyes locked on hers. "More coffee?" he asked.

"Why not?" Bree replied. "I'll come out and help you."

She eased herself out of the tent and stood up. It was warmer and the rain had stopped. Ray had lit a small fire, and the smoke curled up through his flashlight's beam. The aroma of burning wood reached her nostrils. The billy was still half full of bubbling water so she spooned instant coffee and powdered milk into two mugs and poured in the water.

"Biscuit?" Ray said and held out a wrapper of cookies.

"Thanks," Bree replied. She sat on a log and stared at the moths flying in the firelight. Behind was a curtain of darkness. "It's different," she said.

"What is?"

"I was just comparing tonight with last night, that's all. It was quite terrifying, you know."

Ray nodded. "I believe you," he said. "It can be scary, but at other times being out here away from the rat race is one step closer to heaven. I thought I only needed Pattie."

"Past tense?" Bree said.

Ray grinned. "A couple of pleasant English women can make a lot of difference," he said, glanced away and changed the topic. "I think we should head up to the top hut in the morning. That's where I was heading when I heard your plane come down. It'll be a steep climb but we can take it slowly. How's your wound?"

Bree raised her eyes. "Much better. Oh, I know it's there but the throbbing pain has stopped. Your first aid made the difference, I'd say."

"Meanies," interrupted a voice. "You could've made me a drink."

Bree turned to see Jenny and Pattie coming out of the tent. She frowned, chastised herself for being selfish and changed her expression to a smile. Jenny, however, obviously noticed her first expression and gave her a dig on the arm. "Sorry," she whispered. "I didn't mean to interrupt." She grinned. "Beautiful evening, isn't it?"

"I was just telling Ray how scary it was last night," Bree said. She felt her cheeks flush and hoped the dim light hid it.

"Sure," Jenny said in a deadpan voice. "Now, how about that coffee?"

CHAPTER SEVEN

The trio talked for more than an hour during that dark night. Jenny gave a vivid account of the attack on them in her classroom.

"We were just getting over it," she said and ignored Bree's attempts to keep her quiet. "That's why poor old Bree has had so much trouble. She was pretty bruised, you know."

"Jenny, "Bree finally said in exasperation. "Will you shut up?"

"No, I'm interested," Ray said. "How did you know Jenny was being attacked, Bree, or did you just happen to be in the right place at the right time?"

"Like Pattie and you being here to hear our aeroplane come in?" Bree said.

"I guess."

"We had new security cameras installed throughout the school. I was just leaving when an alarm went off. They ignore normal conditions but are activated by sudden movement, smoke or loud noises."

"And I was fair screaming," Jenny added. "God, I was terrified." She screwed her nose up and gave Pattie a hug. "It seems so remote from here, though. There's peace in this valley."

"Oh, we have our share of problems in the back country," Ray said. "Just because it's remote doesn't mean the nasties in society go away."

"Like what?" Bree asked.

Ray glanced up at her. "Oh, the hunters and trampers are usually okay. Some are loners and look mighty scruffy, but beneath their outward appearance they're harmless enough. It's the criminal element that you have to be careful of."

"But why would they be out here?" Bree said.

"Drugs. Marijuana is a banned crop in New Zealand, as I guess it is in England, yet we have one of the highest usage rates in the western world."

"All grown illegally?" Jenny asked.

"Yeah. There are some highly sophisticated plots with tripwires and booby traps to keep strangers out." He shrugged. "Don't worry, they're further down in the lowlands and within a day's walking distance of a road. Only professional hunters come this far back. That's why the huts are better up here."

"How do you mean?" Bree asked.

"The ones up here are appreciated and looked after. Closer to the road they are often vandalized, with graffiti strewn about and stuff taken. Those more than a day's walking distance from a road are respected more. If you agree, we'll head up to Taylor's Mistake Hut tomorrow. It's near the stream so if any search planes come over we can still try to attract their attention. Searchers on foot could be heading in by now, too."

"Taylor's Mistake? That's a strange name," Jenny said.

"An early pioneer thought there was gold in these hills. He disappeared and turned up months later half crazy with a story of a vein of gold. Others went looking but found nothing, hence the name."

"A bit like fool's gold in those old cowboy films?" Jenny said.

Ray tossed a stick on the fire and nodded. "Some copper was discovered and mined but there was never enough to be profitable. They even named a creek Copper Mine Creek further down near the Manawatu Gorge. There are still a few old ruins around. You know, holes in the hill, a few railway sleepers and rusting machinery. It's covered in creeper and almost impossible to find now. The area is steeped in history. Farms were set up but the cleared land was of poor quality and was too cold in winter. They were all abandoned and the bush grew back. There's a spot only a few hours walk from here where there are a dozen old apple trees. The early settlers planted them. In spring, hundreds of daffodils come out."

"So we'll head for this hut tomorrow," Bree said. "How far is it?"

"Five hours. Perhaps longer."

"And what's the other way?" Jenny added.

"There's another hut, the one I set out from. We could go that way but it'll take longer."

"But won't we have to go back that way, anyway?" Bree asked.

"No," Ray replied. "Taylor's Mistake is the most remote hut, that's true, but from there we can go down the eastern side of the ranges and out into farm land. Mind you, I wouldn't be surprised if we run into search teams before then. Whatever happens, we should be out before the end of the weekend and you can catch up with your conference."

"Yes," Bree replied with a sigh. "That doesn't seem very important anymore."

She finished her drink and crawled back into the tent. Jenny and Pattie followed. Bree noticed Ray sit down with his back against a tree trunk. "Come in," she said. We won't bite."

Ray laughed. "Thanks, I will," he said, tossed some soil on the dying embers and crawled inside. Pattie came up, wriggled in beside him and within a few moments silence fell over the tiny camp as Bree fell asleep.

*

Ray considered himself reasonably fit, but the climb out of the valley stretched his endurance to the limit. The summer storm had gone and, even in the shady undercover, the temperature rose. Perspiration soaked his shirt, and the heavy backpack cut into his shoulders. Furthermore, there was no path or trail, just tree trunks, ferns and supplejack. The black vines that hung from the overhead foliage were both a blessing and a curse. They were strong and could be used like rope to pull up on, but the lower ones tended to trip weary feet if the walkers weren't careful.

Two hours after their early morning start, he called a halt. Jenny wiped perspiration off her face and swatted circling insects. She caught Ray's eyes and her red face changed into a slight smile.

"Bree can't take much more," she said. "I think her ribs are giving her hell."

Ray glanced down through the trees to where Bree was using supplejack to pull herself up to a small knob. The tail wagging Pattie was with her as if to give encouragement. Bree staggered the remaining few metres up to the waiting pair. Ray leaned forward, grabbed her arm and helped her up the last section.

"Why didn't you tell us you needed a rest?" he said in a firm but compassionate voice. "You look buggered."

Bree turned towards him and laughed. "Buggered?" she teased.

Ray flushed. "Yeah, well," he muttered. "I forget I've got a couple of English girls with me." He also laughed. "What should I say? 'By jove, old chap, I am somewhat tired.' What?"

"Something like that," Bree replied. "My God, it's hot."

"Yeah, almost thirty," Ray said.

Bree gave an involuntary grunt and squinted as she manipulated into a sitting position and leaned against the bank.

"Does it hurt?" Ray asked. Both the women impressed him with their stamina, but something about Bree in particular sent tremors through his anatomy. It wasn't that she looked like Maxie, far from it, but her mannerisms and nature were similar. That was it, of course! He was not seeing her as a stranger he happened to stumble upon who would soon disappear from his life as quickly as she came into it.

"What have I done?" Bree's soft voice shook him back to reality.

"Careful, Ray," Jenny cut in. "I reckon Bree knows how to mind read. It's all us neurotic teachers she has to manage every day."

"Jenny!" Bree chastised.

"Well, it's true."

Ray laughed but avoided Bree's eyes. The chatter had helped them all relax a little. "I was just thinking how well you've both done. I've one last bandage in my pack. Would you like me to change the one you have?"

Bree smiled. "No, keep it until later. If you have some cotton wool though."

"Cotton wool coming up," Ray said and reached for his backpack. He gave her the cotton wool, then produced some apples as well, and the group rested before continuing through the trees.

Bree didn't want to admit it, but her wound throbbed, and the climbing didn't help. She welcomed it when Ray dropped back and gave her a hand over a fallen tree trunk that blocked their progress. His help and patience made her compare him to her husband who always managed to belittle her whenever she asked for his help.

"We'll be at the top soon," Ray said. "Once there, we'll follow a ridge along to the right. It should be quite a gentle slope to the top of the bush line."

"Then what?" Bree asked.

"There's a tussock-covered plateau. We cross it, and Taylor's Mistake Hut is back where the bush starts again at the top of the next valley."

They were interrupted by Jenny's shout. Bree looked up and saw her friend standing in sunshine above them.

"I see it," Jenny shouted. "There's a helicopter near the aeroplane wreckage."

Pattie bounded back from Jenny to Ray, across to Bree and back to her master. Her tongue hung out and her tail wagged. Once she decided they were okay, she shot back up to the patch of sunshine where Jenny waited.

"Pattie's fit," Bree puffed. "I reckon by the time she runs up and down between us all she covers twice the distance we do."

"True," Ray replied. "You should see her go if there are rabbits or opossums to chase."

They reached the clearing together to find it was a grass-covered outcrop high above the valley. Way below, the waterfall tumbled over a massive cliff into a lake of frothing water. From there, the water continued down a broad valley meandering through gravel and stones. It was the other side of the outcrop, though, that was interesting. Here, the grass stopped, there were a couple of grey rocks, and then nothing until treetops reached the base of the precipice they were perched on. Across from this they could see the stream again. The silver wing and part of the fuselage of their aeroplane was caught on the outside of a bend. Three people, the size of ants, were examining the wreckage. Further back, a small red helicopter sat on a triangular sandbar.

"We came the wrong way," Jenny said with disappointment in her voice. "They'll never see or hear us up here."

"We had no choice," Bree replied. "Look at that waterfall, Jenny. It would be impossible to climb down those cliffs."

Jenny sucked on her lip. "I know, but if we'd stayed at the crash site?"

"I believe you would have been missed," Ray replied. He took his mobile phone out, then frowned when the instrument still showed they were still out of range. "The floodwaters carried the wreck over the waterfall but wouldn't it have been logical for the plane to have landed below it?" He turned to Bree. "Did your pilot mention the falls?"

Bree frowned. "No, not that I can remember," she replied.

"But if they find only one body, won't they search up above the falls?" Jenny argued.

"Possibly," Ray said. "I doubt if the pilot's body will be in the wreckage, though. If they find it a few kilometres downstream they'll concentrate their efforts on searching in the same area. I doubt if they'd expect anyone to have survived the crash after finding the wreckage in its present condition."

"Okay!" Jenny relented. "But Bree can't take much more..."

"I'm just tired," Bree whispered. "We all are."

"Sure," Jenny replied and stared down the valley. "Look, I believe the helicopter's leaving. We could wave and hope they see us."

However, after the helicopter rose above the downed Cessna, it headed downstream without increasing altitude. "They'll be searching as they go, so will be looking down," Ray predicted as the helicopter disappeared down the valley. "It'll be okay, though. Two hours tops to Taylor's Mistake. I had supplies flown in there for me. It may be isolated but we'll be safe."

Jenny looked at Ray. "It's not that I don't appreciate everything you've done, Ray. It's just that if we weren't here, you'd be alone, wouldn't you?"

"Yes, why?"

"And maybe company is a good thing," she said.

Bree gasped, fully understanding the insinuation. "Stop it Jenny! That was uncalled-for." Anger bubbled in her throat, and she looked again at Ray.

He looked directly at her when he spoke, although he answered Jenny. "What I'd like right now is for that helicopter to appear above us and whip you both out of here. I would be selfish to even consider anything else. I knew that when I accepted the contract, I would be alone."

Bree tried to think of something to say but Jenny beat her to it.

"If I sounded bitchy, I'm sorry. I just...damn... anyway, we have no say in where that helicopter goes, do we?"

"No," Bree said. "But think what we'd be doing right now if Pattie never found us?"

Ray smiled. "Now we're here let's have lunch. I made a thermos of coffee this morning, there are three hard-boiled eggs, a few hard buns and other bits and pieces." He paused. "I won't say that I'm not glad of the company, though."

Bree and Jenny exchanged a glance as Ray prepared lunch.

"Now who can mind read?" Bree whispered.

*

After waiting further in case the helicopter returned, the trio sat off along another ridge. The gradual uphill slope was easy, as was tramping along the small track that they found to follow. Half an hour later, the bush stopped and the trio walked out into bright sunshine. Ahead, as far as they could see was bronze tussock, a spiky grass that grew in clumps. They had reached the top plateau.

It was easier going but new problems soon became apparent. There was no shade at all and it was hot.

Ray took out a tube of sunscreen lotion. "Cover your skin as much as you can," he said. "Without a tan you'll both sunburn far quicker than in Europe. It's got worse over the last few summers. Something to do with the deleted ozone layer in this part of the world."

Bree applied liberal quantities to her skin and watched Jenny do the same before they followed Ray through the ocean of tussock. Despite the heat, Pattie woofed in delight and tore off in every direction after small animals hidden to all but her. Bree's leg muscles were more flexible but her shoulders became sore and she was damp from perspiration.

Ray stopped every few moments to check a compass he had. "We're heading southwest," he said. "We have to be careful, though. It's easy to stroll off in the wrong direction up here."

"It's beautiful up here," Bree commented.

They appeared to be on top of the world. Behind them, three mountains rose above the brown plain. To the west, a silver river meandered through rectangles of land coloured from dark green to yellow and brown. It stretched towards the azure ocean that met the horizon. The bright blue sky was so clear Bree felt she could see forever. The blazing sun was a quarter of the way down its western slope, and she glanced at her watch. It was almost four o'clock.

"How much longer?" Jenny asked. Her face was crimson, and dark rings beneath her eyes showed fatigue. Circles of perspiration saturated her clothing.

Ray turned to a map he pulled from his pocket. "About half an hour's walk to the bush, then it's all downhill in the shade to Taylor's Mistake Hut. An hour and a half, perhaps two."

"You said that at lunchtime," Bree pointed out.

"I know," Ray said, with a small smile. "I didn't want you to get discouraged. Sorry about the deception."

"Okay," Jenny cut in. "But let's get going. I'm beginning to hate this tussock." She wiped her forehead and strutted out ahead of the other two.

"Jenny," shouted Bree. "You're going the wrong way!"

The younger woman turned, saw where Bree was pointing, swore, called Pattie and changed direction.

"She's a good kid," Ray said to Bree as they followed.

"Yes. Our parents were friends and we more or less grew up together. You know, she was a little like a kid sister hanging around. She can be a little stubborn at times but I'm glad she's with me."

Fifteen minutes later, Jenny staggered in mid-stride, sighed and, without any further warning, collapsed onto the ground.

CHAPTER EIGHT

Linda Rourke peered out the window. A police car sat at the curb, and two officers were walking the narrow footpath leading to the front door. Curious, she opened the door before they could knock. "Can I help you, officers?"

"I am Constable Jason Hillthorpe, Madam," the closest officer replied and held out an identity card. "This is Constable Yvonne Dewire. Are we at the residence of Mr. Colin Ashworth?"

"Why, yes," the woman replied. "We were just having a cup of tea. Please come in."

"Thank you, Madam," Hillthorpe said. "And you are?"

"Oh, I'm sorry. My name is Linda Rouke." She turned and called out in a louder voice. "Colin, two police officers wish to speak to you."

A scowling Colin Ashworth stepped into the entranceway and studied the new arrivals. "Is there a problem?" he asked.

"It is a personal matter. We need to speak to you privately, Mr. Ashworth?" Dewire said.

"Anything you have to say can be said in front of Linda. We hold no secrets from each other."

The two officers glanced at each other before Hillthorpe spoke. "Very well, sir," he said. "We have just received a message from the New Zealand Police Department."

Colin frowned but otherwise showed little emotion. "It's about Bree, isn't it?"

"I am afraid so, Mr. Ashworth. She was involved in an aeroplane crash in the central North Island of New Zealand. Three people were on board a light aircraft – the pilot, your wife and Miss Jenny Dench. The body of the pilot has been recovered but your wife and Miss Dench are still missing."

"So, she could be alive?" Colin whispered.

"We don't know, Mr. Ashworth. The New Zealand police said the weather conditions were bad at the time of the crash. The aeroplane made a forced landing in a flooded stream in rugged terrain. They believe both your wife and Miss Dench were killed in the crash and their bodies swept downstream in the floodwaters. Search crews are combing the area at this very moment."

"But have found nothing?" Colin retorted.

"No, sir," Yvonne Dewire replied. "We have been advised that the chances of them surviving is practically nil. I'm sorry. We have a personal number you can call in New Zealand if you wish to speak to the officer on the case there."

"I'll do that," Colin said. He ignored Linda, took the card given to him and disappeared out of the room.

Linda stared at his retreating back. "They were only recently separated," she muttered. "I ... I mean Colin and I moved here from London after the separation." Her hands shook. "Would you like to come through for a cup of tea? "

"Thank you. We'll need to speak to the New Zealand police when Mr. Ashworth has finished so would appreciate a cup," Yvonne replied in a soft voice. "There are also a couple of questions we need to ask."

They walked through to a modernised kitchen where Linda busied herself pouring the tea. Yvonne stayed with her while Jason excused himself and walked through to where Colin's voice could be heard speaking. Both men returned a few moments later.

"It sounds bad," was all Colin said.

*

"Tell me," Yvonne said as she and Jason drove away a few moments later. "Was the atmosphere there somewhat strained or was it my imagination?"

"When you tell someone his wife is missing and presumed dead you'd hardly expect him to be laughing."

"I didn't mean that. It was the interaction between him and the woman." Yvonne shrugged. "Or should I say complete lack of it. If anything, Linda Rouke appeared more affected by the news than Ashworth was."

"I've had to do this a few times," Jason said. "People react differently to tragic news." He stopped the squad car at a set of lights. "I must admit he did seem a somewhat cold character."

"And her condition! Rouke had bruises on her arms."

"You noticed? It sounds typical..."

"What does?"

"A young woman starts an affair with an older guy. Everything is grand until they move in together, then he shows his true colours. If he was prone to violence with his wife he just continues it with the mistress." He glowered at the red light. "Perhaps we could give the London Metro Police a call and see if they have anything on this pair. You've got me curious."

Yvonne nodded. "Did anything new come up from his conversation with the New Zealand police?"

"Not really. The weather over there has cleared and a ground party is searching the river for bodies. Apparently, there's a huge area to cover. I spoke to the chap on the phone and he told me the aeroplane was just a crumbled heap of metal, sliced in half through the fuselage. They'll keep in touch."

"Tragic," Yvonne said. She reached forward as the radio splattered into life. Their next dispatch was coming through. For the moment, Colin Ashworth and his mistress were forgotten.

*

By the time Bree reached her, Jenny lay slumped with eyes closed and a line of froth dribbling down her chin. The places not sunburned, were chalk white. Bree placed a hand on her forehead, the gasped.

"She's burning up."

Ray gave Jenny a quick appraisal. "Heat exhaustion," he said. He slid out of his backpack, found a canteen, poured a little water on the corner of a towel and wiped her face.

"How do you know?"

"Sweating, clammy skin." He straightened. "We need shade. I'll get the tent up."

Bree held Jenny while Ray began erecting the tent. He was fast and, mere moments later, he lifted Jenny into his arms and carried her inside the tent, where he lay her on his unrolled sleeping bag.

"I'll see what there is in my first aid kit," he said.

Bree nodded and sat down near Jenny's head. Ray came up with a small bottle of clear liquid.

"Try this," he said. "It's powerful so don't try sniffing it yourself."

Bree nodded, unscrewed the top and pulled back. My God, it was powerful. The smell akin to ammonia and rotten eggs made her eyes water and she spluttered. She gulped, tipped a little of the fluid on the towel and held it under Jenny's nose.

It worked. Jenny jerked conscious, coughed violently and her eyes bulged. "I'm going..." she groaned and vomited in a basin Ray had produced in anticipation.

Afterwards, she sipped a little water and stared up at her concerned companions. "I'm sorry," she managed to gasp. "God I feel awful."

She was sick again but afterwards a little colour appeared in her face and she took the towel from Bree to wipe her lips.

"Just relax," Bree replied. "Sip a little water if you can. You'll be fine."

Jenny nodded. "I'm, sorry," she apologized again. "One minute I was walking along, the next, the whole world began to spin. Then, I smell that vile stuff you waved under my nose. What is it?"

"Some concoction my grandmother always used," Ray said. "She swore by it. I've always carried some in my medical kit."

Jenny smiled faintly, wiped her eyes and attempted to sit up. "Oh, hell," she gasped and flopped back down. "Everything's spinning."

"Just lie there," Bree said. "You're going nowhere at the moment."

"But..."

"There's no hurry," Ray said. "We'll just stay here until you feel better."

Bree watched as Pattie crept into the tent and flopped down beside Jenny.

Jenny looked up at the dog. "Hi, girl," she said. "I'm a cot case, aren't I?"

Pattie lay down with her chin out along her front paws. Two massive brown eyes stared at the young woman.

"You've a good pal there, Jenny," Ray said. "Pattie is mighty particular about who she befriends. Now, try a little more water if you wish but nothing else."

"Okay," Jenny muttered, took a small sip, and lay back. Her eyes shut and she lapsed into sleep. This time though, her breathing appeared normal and her lips lost their blue hue.

"She should be okay now," Ray said. "Keep the moist towel on her forehead."

"Thanks, Ray," Bree said, then smiled. "You seem to have everything in that backpack of yours."

"I guess," Ray replied. "I'm just a naturally cautious person, I suppose. You can't just stroll out here with a couple of apples in your back pocket and a spare jersey slung around your shoulders." He smiled back.

"So, we'll be okay here?" Bree asked. "It's pretty exposed."

"It's not a good place to spend the night. When it's cooler we should keep going. Once we get back to the bush line, we'll find a sheltered spot and go on to the hut tomorrow." He frowned. "It depends a little on Jenny's condition, of course." He looked across at Bree. "And how are you?"

"Okay," Bree replied. "That steep climb was a killer but out here on the tussock I've coped." She sighed. "It is hot, though."

"And your ribs?"

"Better," Bree replied. "They're sore if I bump them but otherwise okay."

"Good," Ray said. "I'll find us something to eat."

"A never ending supply," Bree said.

"Not quite. We're almost down to raisins and energy bars. There'll be no flash breakfast in the morning." He checked Jenny and slipped out of the tent.

*

Jenny awoke a few moments later and insisted she would be able to walk. However, Ray and Bree insisted she rest until the sun was lower in the sky. When they did move, Jenny had lost her earlier bouncy pace but managed a steady rate across the tussock. It took another hour of walking through the slightly downhill terrain before Ray pointed to trees ahead. He checked his compass, declared they were going in the correct direction and placed an arm around Bree's shoulders.

"It's Jenny who needs a helping hand," Bree said, but never pulled away.

"She's got Pattie," Ray replied. "You're finding it as hard a trek as her, aren't you?"

Bree sighed. "I am tired, yes. How do you manage to keep going? And don't give me any male macho crap." She let her head lean against Ray's shoulders.

"I didn't just survive an aeroplane crash." He glanced down at her and smiled.

As Jenny slipped in beside the pair, Bree glanced at her, flushed and stepped away from Ray.

"It's been a long day," she said. "Are you still okay?"

"Me," Jenny replied. "Apart from a splitting headache, I'm fine. By your looks, better than you, I'd say." She turned to Ray. "I'd like to try to reach the hut, if possible Ray. Will there be time before nightfall?"

Ray glanced at his watch. "It's just after seven, so there's a couple of hours of daylight. Probably a little less once we're back in the bush. We' be cutting it fine but could make it." He turned. "Can you manage, Bree?"

"As long as it's downhill, I can do it," Bree replied. "I wouldn't like another climb, though."

With the end in sight, Bree felt more cheerful. Still, she was exhausted. Jenny never mentioned being tired but her haunted expression showed that she was at the end of her endurance, too. The plateau now sloped downhill and the trio were soon pushing through tall flax that towered over their heads and hid everything from sight. Ray led, and using his tramping boots to push flax and grass aside. He helped everyone, even Pattie, who needed to be lifted over tree stumps that were buried beneath the flax.

"This area was once covered in trees," Ray said. "A hundred and fifty years ago the settlers burned it down but only this secondary growth of flax grew back. In winter, this is quite swampy with water running off the top tussock."

Bree found this new vegetation was far more difficult to walk through. She glanced at Ray but didn't say the words in her mind.

"I didn't realize we'd have to got through this," he said as if he had read her thoughts. "We're further south than I had thought."

"And what does that mean?" Jenny asked.

"Once we're through this flax the distance to the hut will actually be less."

"Shorter?" Bree teased. "Or are you trying to soften the blow? You know, it's 'just around the corner'."

Ray reached out and squeezed her arm. "No, it's true," he said.

He was partly right. It was after nine and twilight when something man-made showed through the foliage.

"Taylor's Mistake Hut," Ray said and Bree sighed in relief. "That's the roof you can see. We've made it, ladies. We've made it, Pattie."

"Woof," the dog barked and ran ahead though the dim light.

Bree smiled and gave Jenny a quick hug. The younger woman glanced up at her. "And they call these things ranges," she whispered. "It makes Wales seem like a London suburb."

*

Taylor's Mistake Hut was a small modern 'A' framed building. The steep roof overhung the front to form a veranda the buildings width. A wooden bench was tucked along the wall under an aluminium-framed window and beside the end door.

Bree walked up the wooden steps, across the veranda floor and pushed the door open. A smell of wood and smoke caught her nose as she stepped in. On the left, under the low exposed beams, a wooden bench, cupboards and kitchen sink were tucked next to a freestanding iron stove. A steel, cylindrical chimney poked up though the roof. A table and tubular steel chairs filled the centre of the room, while the right side held a sofa, one armchair and a low bench with some magazines and books stacked on it. The living quarters took up over half the hut's area. Three adjacent doors dominated a dividing wall and a small ladder led up to a mezzanine space above the end rooms, where two packs and several cardboard boxes were stacked.

"Good, my supplies are here," Ray said from the entrance door.

Bree walked forward and pushed the left door open. Inside was a tiny bunkroom with a low ceiling, four bunks along one wall and a row of push-open windows above them. Mattresses were tipped sideways on each bunk. At the far end, another door probably led outside. The right door had another bunkroom that was a mirror image of the first, while the central door led to two narrow doors that slid open across each other. Inside were two cubicles; one contained a shower, while the second had a flush toilet and minute washbasin.

"Oh my God," Bree whispered. "I never expected this."

Ray smiled. "The hut parts were flown in by helicopter and bolted together a year ago. I believe the original one it replaced was over a hundred years old. There's a septic tank and water supply fed from a stream further up the hill. There's no electricity but once the stove is lit we'll have hot water in about three-quarters of an hour. If you can wait that long, you can have a hot shower."

The relief of being able to relax showed in all their faces. Jenny sat on the couch and removed her shoes and socks to reveal massive blisters covering her feet. She glanced at her sunburned, scratched legs, then across to Bree.

"Don't laugh," she said. "You should see your face. I reckon you could cook toast on it."

Bree wiped a hand over her stinging brow. "My leg muscles are worse," she admitted. "If we had to go further they'd have seized up, I'm certain."

"How are your bruised ribs?" Ray asked. He'd also removed his boots but appeared unaffected by his ordeal.

"Sore," Bree admitted. "The bandage is filthy but I'll leave it until I've cleaned up."

Ray smiled. "I'll get the stove lit, otherwise there'll be no hot water."

Bree and Jenny helped with chores so that, by the time darkness descended on Taylor's Mistake Hut, a large kerosene lamp flickered away from a crossbeam hook. The fire was almost too hot but fresh food bubbled away. Bree told Jenny to have the first shower, and she disappeared with some of Ray's borrowed clothes under her arm. She returned ten minutes later wearing his shirt like a dress, and little else.

"Your turn," she said to Bree. "If you toss your clothes out, I'll wash them."

"All of them?" Bree replied doubtfully.

"Oh, don't be a prude," Jenny retorted then grinned. "I'm sure Ray doesn't mind."

It wasn't Bree but Ray who flushed. Bree noticed he avoided glancing at Jenny's ample portions outlined beneath the shirt. He suddenly muttered something about chopping some wood and disappeared outside with Pattie.

"Jenny," Bree gasped. "Did you have to?"

"What?"

"You know! Poor Ray didn't know which way to look when you walked in."

Jenny turned serious. "It's not me he keeps looking at," she said. "After that violent husband of yours, I reckon he's the best thing to happen to you in years." Her eyes widened. "The feeling's mutual isn't it?"

"Jenny," Bree retorted. "Stop it!" She stood and walked towards the steamy shower. "You can come and get my clothes if you wish but, for God's sake don't go parading them around."

"No, Mrs. Ashworth," Jenny replied in an innocent voice and gave a mock salute.

In spite of herself, Bree had to laugh. "Okay," she said. "Point taken. You could put a jersey over that shirt, though."

"Oh, can't stand the competition," Jenny replied and grinned warmly as Bree slid the shower door shut.

*

Bree slept better than any time since her arrival in New Zealand but woke early to find the sun streaming in through the top window. Along the bunkroom, Jenny snored peacefully. Bree glanced at her watch. Even though it was only a little after five-thirty she decided to get up. As expected, the living quarters were empty. Not even Pattie was around. Bree gathered some wood from the woodbin and lit the fire. Next, she checked their washing and found it all dry, so she went back into the bunkroom and dressed in her own clothes.

Still the only one awake, she slipped outside and wandered along a different trail from the way they'd come. This one followed the edge of the hillside and opened out onto a sunny, grassy section. As she walked, her mind wandered. Everything that had happened passed through her mind but her thoughts kept shifting back to the tall New Zealander who had rescued them. He was quiet yet confident, supportive and understanding, a man who had had his own tragedy in life but didn't dwell it. When they talked it was as if he was genuinely interested in her life and wasn't just being polite. What a contrast to Colin! Oh they'd had their good times but it had gradually lost its appeal. Perhaps if they'd had children but two miscarriages in as many years made this almost impossible.

Perhaps she had changed. After the second miscarriage, she had her first real disagreement with Colin. She thought back to that time eight years earlier. It wasn't a disagreement but a full heated argument that was the first of many more.

*

"I am going back to teaching, Colin," she said that fateful morning. "There are always vacancies at schools around London."

Colin turned from the dresser where he was tying his tie. "Why?" he asked. "I make enough money for us both. You have a nice house, a new car and your volunteer groups. What else do you need?"

"Lots," Bree replied. "I loved teaching and would still be doing it if it wasn't for my pregnancy problems."

"We can try again."

"Colin," Bree retorted. "You know what the gynaecologist said. You were there when she explained everything in minute detail."

"Okay," Colin replied. "Anyhow, that's a different issue. To put it frankly, I don't want any wife of mine working."

"But I did when we were first married."

"Yes, to help pay the mortgage and get this house you're standing in. You're damned lucky you know. Not many women in their twenties have a home in a good London borough and all the money they need."

"Yes, but I almost have to beg if I want anything. Everything, actually."

"Oh rubbish," Colin snapped back. "You only need to ask and I write out a cheque. Look what you've got; the new car I mentioned, clothes galore, new furniture, at least two holidays a year..."

"That's it," Bree blazed back. "Why should I have to ask? You never ask me when you go and buy something. You just turn up with it, even stuff for me; the new dishwasher for example."

"But you needed it. The old one was worn out."

"You don't get it Colin. The point is we never discuss things; you just go and do it but if I want the smallest thing I need to ask. God, Colin, it's not the sixties. You're trying to relive how your father acted."

"All right," Colin said in a quieter voice. "I'll give you an allowance in addition to the housekeeping money. You can spend it how you want."

"And that will solve all our problems, I suppose," Bree added bitterly.

Colin's face darkened. "It's not my fault you can't carry children," he said.

"But your behaviour is," Bree whispered.

"Meaning?"

"You know our sex life is almost nonexistent, Colin." She bit on her bottom lip. "I know about Shelly Carmichael..."

"How?" Colin asked. "We've been..." He clamped his lips tight as if he realized he'd said too much.

Bree stared and, in spite of an earlier promise to herself to remain calm and in control of her emotions, tears formed in her eyes.

"I suspected," she said. "Then Shelly came to see me. Sexy bit isn't she? Trouble is her background is similar to yours, you know, strict Anglican upbringing..."

Colin's frown became deeper but he said nothing.

"She seems to think I'm the only one preventing a quickie divorce, your remarriage to her and happiness ever after... in this house, of course."

"Damned lies," Colin snorted.

"Who from, Shelly or you?" Bree cut back. "And don't deny you've been having an affair with her for months now; about the time of my miscarriage, I'd say."

"So what about you?" the man retorted. "You've acted like a bitch for months. At least Shelly shows a little affection. If you acted more like a wife, I wouldn't have to go out to get satisfaction elsewhere."

Bree wiped her tears away. "So I need something else, Colin. That's why I'm going to apply for one of those teaching vacancies." She gulped. "I'm not asking you, I'm telling you. As for Shelly, if you want to move out and live with her, do it. Don't expect me to leave this house, though. Remember, it was the money I inherited when Dad died that paid for most of the deposit."

"You bitch," Colin replied.

His eyes were beyond anger now. In one movement, he stepped forward and slapped her across the face. The action was so violent, her head jerked back and blood poured from a split lip.

She recovered, stepped back and held a handkerchief to her mouth. "Do that again, Colin and I'll ask my lawyer to file an assault charge against you," she whispered, fury heating her words. "Think what that'll do to your precious social standing and career."

She flung her head back, turned and walked out of the room.

CHAPTER NINE

Bree watched two fantails chasing tiny insects in the sunlight. One flew almost within an arm's length from her, landed on a branch and cocked its head. It seemed completely unafraid as its tail feathers fanned out to illustrate how it got its name.

Rustling in the undergrowth made her apprehensive for a second until Pattie bounded into sight and ran up to her, tail thumping. A moment later, Ray appeared, fully dressed in work boots, shorts and tartan jacket.

"Hi Bree," he said. "Pattie's missed her morning walks over the last couple of days. We've been out for about twenty minutes. I thought I'd come back and light the fire. I saw smoke from the chimney and wondered if it was you. Sleep well?"

Bree smiled. "I did." She glanced around. "Aren't those little fantails delightful?"

"Yes," Ray said. He kicked at a clump of dirt. "I was by a minute ago, but you seemed immersed in thought. Are you worried about that conference you're missing?"

"No," Bree said. "I'd rather be here. For the first time in years, I've stepped back and looked at my life. Out here, I can become almost detached." Bree glanced up. "I've told you most of the things about my ex-husband. I was just thinking back to when it all began. His first affair was with a girl named Shelly Carmichael. Funny, I hardly knew the woman but the name is embossed in my mind."

"And what happened to her?"

"She got serious and Colin dropped her." Bree sighed. "Poor girl. I almost felt sorry for her at the time. I met her a few months back. She came up like a long lost friend. She's married with a couple of kids... seems happy, too." Bree told Ray about that first confrontation with Colin.

"So, you went back teaching?" Ray said when she finished.

"Yes, the next term. I've been back ever since. Oh, Colin got used to it. The only other big row was when I won the headteacher's job at Sunset Grove." She chuckled. "The salary I was offered was higher than his. It shot hell out of his pride. That was when he started having affairs again. In his warped mind, he had to prove his manliness, I guess."

"Cowardliness, more like it," Ray said. "You're better off without him."

"Yes. My only regret is I should have done it eight years ago. I partly blamed myself. I guess I thought he'd change but he never did." She chuckled. "He had to swallow his pride a couple of years back when he was made redundant and I supported him for three months."

"Did he appreciate it?"

"Not really. That's when he started his clandestine affair with Linda Rouke. She was number three, but there were probably others."

"So, what did you do?"

"Immersed myself in my work. Teaching can take your whole life if you let it." She laughed. "That's why I don't mind missing the conference. There'll always be another one."

"Fair enough," Ray replied and crouched down by the log to pat Pattie.

Bree watched him, her thoughts racing. One part of her wanted him to move across and tuck his arms around her, while another drew back in anticipation of how she'd react if he made such a move. It didn't matter, though, as Ray straightened, remaining out of physical contact range.

"Breakfast?" he asked.

"Excuse me?" Bree shook aside the daydream.

"I have mushrooms, bacon and eggs for breakfast." He chuckled again.

Bree nodded. "It sounds wonderful, Ray, but I'll do the cooking. It's the least I can do. Okay?"

"We both can." He turned to Pattie. "I think I can find a bone for you, too, girl," he said. "Won't that be grand?"

Pattie's response was immediate. She gave a bark and ran towards the hut.

"So what happens today?" Bree asked as they walked back at a more leisurely pace.

"That's up to you, but I have one suggestion."

"And that is?"

"It's a five hour tramp to the next hut and another three hours to the closest road on that side. I think you should both spend the day recuperating."

"But that doesn't include you?" Bree said.

Ray smiled. "That hill to our west is the last major obstacle before the Manawatu Plains. There's another ravine beyond so we can't get out that way."

"But you're still thinking of going there?"

Ray nodded. "Once I'm at the summit, I'll be able to use the mobile phone to call in a rescue team. A helicopter could be here within half an hour."

"I see," Bree replied. She should have been elated but her stomach felt sort of flat.

"You don't sound very enthusiastic about a rescue, Bree."

Bree flushed, coming up a flimsy excuse. "I'm worried. The hill looks steep. Will you be able to make it?"

"I'll take Pattie and plenty of gear. The map I was studying shows a ridge that cuts up the north side. I probably wouldn't even need to go as far as the ridge since the hill curves southwest. If the transmission tower on Whariti Peak comes into sight, I'll make my call and return. The whole trip will take three hours at the most. If I leave after breakfast, I'll be back by lunchtime."

"Better still, get the helicopter to pull you off, too."

"I suppose I could do that..."

"Take care, Ray. Don't take any risks. If the terrain is too difficult, come back and we'll walk out together tomorrow."

Ray placed an arm around her shoulders for a second and smiled. "It's nice to have someone who cares," he whispered. "Somehow these ranges will seem empty without you."

"Really?' Bree replied.

Ray glanced down at her and smiled. "Yes, really," he replied.

*

"Look, I'll be okay," Ray repeated half an hour later outside the hut. He slipped his backpack over his jacket and whistled up Pattie. "I've got the route sketched on the map I left on the table. If there are any messages I'll tell the rescue crew. The helicopter could be here before I get back,"

"So why don't you come back, too?" Bree asked.

Ray smiled. "I work here remember. There's work to do." He studied Bree's face. "Okay, I've the name of the motel you're booked into in Palmerston North and you've got my mobile number."

"Which won't reach you here," Jenny cut in.

"We don't want to just disappear from your life," Bree added. "It's not fair after all you've done. Can't you come back with us if we're rescued." She pouted. "You did say you were ahead in your work. What difference will a couple of days make?"

Ray smiled. "Okay," he said. "When I contact the rescue chopper, I'll ask them to pick me up."

"Good," Bree said and walked into the hut so she didn't have to watch Ray disappear through the trees.

A moment later, Jenny came in and stood beside her. "He'll be okay," she said. "He's used to tramping through the bush."

"We should have gone with him," Bree said.

"Oh, Bree," Jenny replied. "His reasoning was sound. You admitted your ribs still hurt." She grimaced. "After yesterday, I'd be more of a hindrance than a help anyway."

"I guess," Bree replied. "I can't help feeling everything isn't as simple as Ray painted, that's all."

"God, Bree, you're acting like a love smitten teenager." Jenny ducked away as if she expected a clout from Bree but there was no reaction. "Damn," she added. "It's worse than I thought."

"It's nothing," Bree finally said. "He's a nice guy who rescued us, that's all."

"Yeah, so you said yesterday," Jenny replied. "Come on. What say we use some of Ray's supplies to cook up a nice meal?" She smiled. "It's better than just moping around."

"And you keep out of the sun," Bree warned. "Your sunburn looks terrible."

*

The day moved on and apprehension turned to worry when mid-afternoon came and went. They had the map he'd left, of course, but it was not sufficiently detailed to show trails. The contour lines were close together, indicating the higher points were as steep, if not steeper than the hill they'd had so much trouble climbing the day before.

Bree stood in the living room packing items in one of the backpacks that came with Ray's supplies. "Just in case," she said when Jenny asked what she was doing. "Anyhow, it gives me something to do."

"Listen!" Jenny said and glanced outside. "Isn't that Pattie barking?"

"My God, it is." Bree flung the backpack aside and almost ran out the door, Jenny following.

She was only a few metres up the path when Pattie appeared out of the distant shrubbery. The dog was limping and covered in mud. Her eyes looked mournful and the long tail dragged along the ground. When she saw Jenny, her tail gave several wags before she yelped and broke into a run. Seconds later, she almost leapt into Jenny's arms, before dropping back with a whine.

"What is it, girl?" Jenny asked. "Where's Ray?"

Pattie's whine turned to a bark. She turned and ran back up the path, stopped and returned. Jenny followed a short distance, only to return a moment later.

"Ray's not here," she said. "But I think Pattie wants us to follow."

Bree gasped. "Oh my, I knew something would happen. I'm going to find Ray."

"Okay, but wait one moment," Jenny replied. "Finish packing the backpacks. We'll need the tent, food, water and the first aid kit. Those warmer clothes you packed were a good idea."

It was the younger woman who now became the one in charge. She opened a tin of dog food and poured some water in a basin for Pattie. The dog lapped the water up in several slurps and ate the food before glancing up. Her tail began to wag as if she knew help was on its way.

"And we eat something, too," Jenny said as Bree paced back and forth along the veranda with the largest backpack on her back. "I'll write a note to leave on the table."

"Of course," Bree responded. "I should have thought of that." Her voice rose. "The map! Where's the map!"

"In my pocket," Jenny responded. She grabbed the hut's logbook and scribbled a note on the first blank page.

Bree watched as Jenny found some of Ray's clothes and poked them into the second backpack. "Oh, Jenny," she cut in and rushed to help. "I'm sorry. I should have thought of that, too."

Jenny gave a fleeting smile. "I'll forgive you, Mrs. Ashworth," she responded, then studied Bree a moment. "You've got it bad, haven't you?"

Bree stopped and stared at her friend. "Oh Jenny," she said. "My facade has crumbled, hasn't it?"

"So, what if it has, Bree? Shall we go?" Bree nodded and Jenny turned to the dog. "Find Ray, girl," she said. "Keep us in sight. We won't be as fast as you. Understand?"

Pattie did. She ran ahead and stopped at the shrubs. After the pair followed her through, she ran on to the next obstacle, a grove of ferns and waited again. It was a hectic pace but Bree did not even slow. They pushed through supplejack, around logs, over boulders and pulled themselves up the steep hillside.

Jenny was soon gasping for breath but never complained. Pattie stopped after one hard climb through horrible cutting grass that scratched arms, legs and paws.

"Go on, girl," Bree panted. She squinted ahead and wiped perspiration from her eyes.

The dog glanced up at Bree and stood with her head turned and tail drooped. Finally, Jenny appeared from behind them. Her body heaved and sweat-drenched hair covered her mud-splattered face.

"Don't wait," she gasped. "I'll follow."

"No," Bree replied. "Anyhow, Pattie refuses to move. I'm sorry for being selfish. We stick together." She glanced at her watch. "We've been going almost an hour. I think we should have a rest and a drink."

"Thanks,' Jenny gasped. She pulled herself up beside Bree and sat down. "Remember Pattie."

"I will," Bree whispered. "Her pan is in your pack."

*

Forty minutes later the gasping pair came out of the trees onto a ledge bathed in sunshine. The whole hillside had slipped away into a valley below. Grey and white dust, larger slabs of solid chunks assembling concrete, and uprooted trees scarred the hillside. It appeared solid but water trickled from several cracks in the surface.

"Some slip," Jenny gasped. "It looks recent."

"And look," Bree said. "Ray's footprints. He's gone across."

She was about to step forward when Jenny grabbed her arm. "No, we'll rope ourselves together first."

Pattie, though, had a different idea. She raised her head and howled, cocked her ears forward and howled again.

"Listen!" Bree whispered. She frowned and stared down the slip face.

All was quiet. Even Pattie stopped and sat down, saliva pouring from her tongue. Far below a voice called out.

"Ray!" Bree screamed. "Ray. We're here!" She grabbed a branch and leaned out as far as possible but only the slip showed. "Ray!" she screamed again.

Jenny shouted and Pattie howled. They stopped and listened.

"Be careful," a far off voice filtered up from way below. More indecipherable words followed.

Pattie yelped and bounded diagonally down the slip. Even her small size sent rubble moving. The dog went into a dust slide for several metres, recovered, barked again and disappeared out of view.

"We'll still use the rope," Jenny said.

Bree nodded. "If we make our way down beside the slip rather than the face itself..."

She worked with Jenny to find a way down the steep face. On their side of the slip, small, flowering manuka trees covered the hillside. They crawled beneath them but found their backpacks caught on low branches. Bree swore, slid her pack off and dragged it behind. The manuka grove was a world of reddish trunks the size of her hands. A strong but pleasant aroma permeated the air, coming from creamy white flowers. She turned and used the trunks like a ladder to make her way down while Jenny followed. Without the gap of sunlight over the slip to their left, she would have become lost within moments.

It was steep, with the trees often so close together she had to squeeze through or around them. The soil beneath her feet crumbled easily, and often it was only by gripping trunks that she stopped herself from plunging down steep sections. She continued, the silence broken only by Jenny's puffing. A steep, eight-metre drop appeared but below this, the hillside sloped at a more leisurely angle.

"Your rope, Jenny," Bree said. She wiped sticky hands on her clothes and managed to stand upright. "God, my back aches."

After tying the rope end somewhat unprofessionally, but securely, to a manuka trunk, Bree tossed the coil down. She dropped her backpack after it and grinned at Jenny. "Want to go first?"

Jenny shook her head.

Bree grabbed the rope, leaned back over the edge and made her way gingerly out. She kept her legs spread wide as she walked backwards down the slope. At an almost vertical section her confidence wavered. The rope slipped through her hands and she crumbled in a heap on the ground three metres below.

She grimaced and opened her fingers. Blood oozed from diagonal grazes across both hands. Rope burns! One knee was also bleeding and her left upper arm was raw.

"You okay?' Jenny called from above.

Bree glanced up at the dirty concerned face. "Yeah," she called back. "I was trying to be too smart, that's all. I'll hold this end of the rope for you."

Jenny gripped the rope and made a more successful hand-over-hand descent down to Bree. She also wiped sticky hands on her clothes and looked up. Pattie had arrived. "Hi, girl," she panted. "How far now?"

"Ray!' Bree called. "Where are you?"

"Over here!" Ray's voice was still quite a way off but was now parallel to them. "I'm stuck, I'm afraid. Got caught in a landslide."

"Coming," Bree shouted. She hitched the backpack on and headed for the open space ahead. At the edge of the slip, she stopped and took stock. They were about halfway down the face. The cliff they'd just descended extended out onto the slip where it disappeared beneath the rubble of the slip itself. Further out, something moved!

She saw an arm waving. There appeared to be nothing else. Just one arm of Ray's familiar tartan jacket waved out.

"We see you," Bree screamed and moved forward.

CHAPTER TEN

Though Bree was frantic to get out to Ray, common sense came to the fore and she discussed their best approach with Jenny. They toiled with the idea of bringing the rope down but this would cut off the only way back up the cliff.

"Keep together and go straight out," Jenny said. "It's as good a way as any. It looks dry and reasonably solid."

"I agree," Bree replied. "I'll get the medical kit but I think we should leave the backpacks here."

Jenny nodded. "There's another shorter rope here. It could come in handy." She took it from her backpack, tied the rope around Bree's waist, then around herself, and grinned at Pattie who was back beside them. "Go to Ray, girl. We're right behind." She turned to Bree. "You're the leader. Away you go."

The walk across the slip was more of a psychological worry than actual danger, for the view stretched down to the valley hundreds of metres below. Bree stepped cautiously through loose rubble with her gaze darting between places to put her feet and Ray. All she could see was his arm and that was now still. Pattie kept pace with them by zigzagging around uphill with her nose down and tail again wagging.

"Hi, wonderful ladies," Ray said when they came in sight. "We have a wee problem here." He attempted a smile but it became a grimace of pain. "I'm busted up a bit, I'm afraid."

"Oh my, Ray," Bree said and rushed the last few steps, Jenny close behind. She kneeled down, worry furrowing her brow.

Ray was caught under a pile of the grey rocks. Only his head, one shoulder and left arm were exposed. Scorings around his free arm showed where he'd tried to dig himself out. Above them was the evidence of a secondary slip that had caught him.

"I slipped and half the bloody hill came with me." He grimaced. "Something snapped. I think it's my leg."

"Okay," Bree said. "We'll see what we can do." She and Jenny began scooping debris out of the way. "God, we wondered what happened. I wanted to come earlier but Jenny said we'd never find you. She was right, of course, but when Pattie arrived we..." She flung up a hand to brush hair away from her eyes and continued scraping and rambling on, not even conscious of her own words.

"Bree," Ray interrupted. "Come here!"

Bree stopped, sat back and frowned. "What do you mean? I am here."

"Closer," Ray whispered and winked at Jenny. Bree frowned and bent forward.

"What's wrong?'" she said and gazed at his face.

Ray tucked his free arm about her, pulled her close, and placed a tiny kiss on her lips. "Slow down," he whispered. "I'm okay. Really I am."

Bree pulled back, flushing. "Why did you do that?" she gasped, then noticed the strange look that crossed his face. "I'm sorry. I didn't mean... I mean I'm honoured but..."

"Bree, we're almost within range," Ray mumbled.

"Of what?"

"The mobile phone. That's how I got into this mess in the first place. The light on it flickered and, for a second, stayed green."

"Where's your mobile, Ray?" cut in Jenny.

"With the backpack. When I felt myself go, I managed to toss them both away and scream at Pattie to move. It's up there somewhere."

"I'll look," Jenny said and undid the rope that was still attached to Bree. "Come on, Pattie."

"Be careful," Bree said. She turned back to Ray. "What's the best way I can help?"

Ray smiled. "There's a ton of dirt on my chest and it hurts like hell. I think some ribs are cracked. If you could try to remove some..."

Bree crawled above Ray. She used legs as well as arms to push the grey powdery soil aside until she hit something more solid. "There's a boulder buried here," she gasped. "If we can get that out..." Again she worked frantically to push soil away, then glanced up as Jenny half-slid in beside them.

"Found it," she puffed. "Doesn't work, though. There's nothing!"

Bree groaned.

"Take the battery out and clean the connections," Ray suggested, then suddenly added, "Bugger!"

"What is it?" Bree said and grabbed his hand.

"My right side was numb," Ray said. "There's a bit of space there so I moved my foot. Trouble is, when I did, spasms of pain shot up my leg. "

"That's a good sign," Jenny said.

"Yeah," Ray said. He spluttered and tears formed in his eyes. "Did you bring any water across with you."

"Oh my, of course. Why didn't I think..." Bree stood up and reached for their medical kit.

"Because you're trying to do everything," Jenny said. "Look, have a break and let me do some digging."

"No, I want to help," Bree said.

The pair scooped and heaved soil aside. Even Pattie got in the act and did a wonderful job of scratching debris away. As the large boulder came into sight Bree could see what happened. A buried tree trunk formed a small triangular space above Ray's chest and right arm. Further back, his legs were completely covered in soil.

"You can thank the tree trunk, Ray," Bree panted as she scooped an armload of soil aside. "Without this, that boulder would have squashed you completely. Now if we can lift it from that side it should topple away from you."

"We could use the rope to help," Jenny added. "I'll dig Ray's legs out first. If the boulder's too heavy to topple, we could wedge something under it, and Ray might just be able to wriggle out."

"Keep Pattie uphill," Ray said. "I'd hate anything to roll on her." His face was bathed in sweat and every so often he'd grit teeth and swallow saliva.

"More water, Ray?" Bree asked and held a plastic bottle to his lips when he nodded.

By the time they had increased the hole around the boulder sufficiently to wedge a small branch beneath, the sun had reached the hilltops and they were in shadow. The cooler temperature was welcome as they worked. Ray became silent and lapsed into a semi-conscious state.

"It won't work," Bree said a few moments later.

"Why?" gasped Jenny. She was using her fingers to move soil from Ray's legs.

"Look," Bree said. "That leg is all wrong. There's an obvious break. If we try to pull him out we could do more damage to his leg. I think the boulder is leaning the wrong way, too."

"I know," Jenny replied.

Bree sighed in disappointment as she examined the boulder. If she levered the end with the branch and it slipped, it would fall on Ray's chest, not away from him. The weight dropping on him could crush his whole upper body.

"It'll be dark in an hour," she said. "I need to do something else." She stood and stepped over to the mobile phone Jenny had placed in a backpack pocket. "I'm going to call for help."

"But it's not working."

"So I'll move up the slope until I get into range."

Jenny nodded. "Take Pattie. I'll stay with Ray, unless you'd like me to come, too."

"No," Bree replied. "I don't want Ray left alone. You could go and get the tent if it starts getting cooler. We're hot but Ray looks so pale."

"One, one, one," Ray said in almost a croak.

Bree spun around and stared at him. "Sorry, Ray. I thought you were asleep. What did you say?"

"The emergency number in New Zealand is triple one. I think that is different from yours at home?"

"I'll get help, Ray," Bree whispered, squeezed his hand and walked away.

*

When there is a crisis the person waiting often becomes more worried than the one doing something. This was how it was with Jenny. She placed a rolled-up bunch of clothes beneath Ray's head and wiped his face with a damp cloth. He smiled, chatted for a while and dropped asleep again.

She sat watching Bree and Pattie's disappearing forms until the pair were out of sight, then munched absently on an apple as her thoughts drifted back. Suddenly, she jerked up. That man who attacked her at school. She knew him! Well, not personally but she had seen him before.

It was during the Set One Folk Dance evening held the week before the attack. The Year One, Two and Three classes had this annual event where each class put on three dances, there were a couple of grand items and the evening concluded with a grand dance where parents were asked to join in,

One dance consisted of two circles with males on the outside. Everyone danced with the adjacent partner and moved on to the next person at the end of each movement. She mainly had her tiny pupils as a partner but there were a few men in the circle. This man was one. She remembered being embarrassed as he'd said nothing but had gripped her far too close as they swung around. She'd been relieved when she moved on to her next partner, one of the little boys from Badger Room.

Afterwards, she knew the man's gaze followed her, so she purposely retreated to the kitchen where parents were arranging supper.

"Oh my God," she gasped out loud. "It was all premeditated and Bree had to suffer because of me."

"What?" Ray asked.

Jenny grimaced. "Hi, Ray," she said. "You dozed off and I was deep in thought. The guy who attacked me and Bree at school planned his attack on me."

"Bree told me a bit about it. She said he wasn't caught."

"That's right. I thought he was a stranger but now I remember..." She told Ray about the dance episode. "During supper I remember he was watching me. It was creepy. Afterwards I was involved in getting all the kids ready to go home and forgot about him. I never even remembered when he came to the door that afternoon claiming he was Jamie's father. Jamie's one of my pupils. But, a moment ago, it all rushed back into my mind." She bit on her lip. "I never encouraged him at all but it'll look as if I did."

"Why? Did you say anything to him?" Ray replied.

Jenny paled. "No, not really, but he did speak to me."

"What did he say?"

"As everyone left he walked by and said, 'You're a great dancer, Ms Dench. See you sometime.' I remember he stared at..." Jenny flushed. "...more than just my face."

"Tell the police when you get home. With a description, it shouldn't be too hard to find him."

"I know," Jenny said, "But I feel even more responsible for Bree getting involved."

"Don't be," Ray replied. "Bree wouldn't think that for a moment."

Jenny turned her gaze towards Ray. "You're attracted to her aren't you?"

Ray looked away. "Just circumstances, Jenny. You know what it's like when people meet in stressful situations." He laughed. "In a hospital I reckon every male patient falls for the nurse who looks after him, unless they're built like a battleaxe, that is."

"No," Jenny replied. "I think it's more than that, from Bree's point of view, anyway. I've no idea how you feel." She caught Ray's eyes again. "I'm sorry. I'm just being a busy body, that's all."

Ray grinned. "I don't know how I feel either." He wriggled, grimaced in pain and added. "Have you any water left?"

"I think so," Jenny replied. She stood and reached across to where the plastic bottle had been placed by the backpack.

*

In front of Bree and Pattie, the distant hills looked a dark blue above the grey slip face. A line of dark green undergrowth showed to the right. This was where she decided to go. If she got to the corner it could be in line of site of Wharite Peak, the highest hill in the district. On Wharite was a television transmission tower that also held the mobile phone relay stations. Anyway, that's what Ray had told her earlier.

She moved on, her gaze darting between the distant trees and the dog. Not once did she glance down into the valley nor did she turn back to view Ray and Jenny. The soil was so loose she sank in up to her ankles and left grotesque footprints behind. She swallowed any remaining pride and sank to her knees. Now half crawling and half 'spider walking' with hands and feet working in unison, she moved diagonally across the slope.

After twenty minutes, the edge seemed just as far away as when she had left. It was only when she finally stopped and glanced back that she realized that the waving Jenny was way below her.

"Well, Pattie," she said. "We've come a long way after all."

Pattie placed her nose on Bree's knees and gazed up with large brown eyes.

"You've done so much, girl," Bree said and patted Pattie. "You came back to us, led us here, helped us dig Ray out and now you're looking after me." She cuddled the Labrador in her arms and blinked back tears. "I love you, Pattie. Come on!" she said.

The next section was steep but the ground became solid with stunted shrubs growing on it. It appeared she was now on an older slip. The thick undergrowth and trees were also close but the shadows became longer as twilight arrived. She'd been climbing for close to an hour. If nothing happened within the next hour she'd be stuck on the slip face until morning. It would be too dangerous to return to the others in the dark.

"Goddamn hills," she cursed and yanked the mobile phone out for the umpteenth time. She pressed the on switch and a green light shone. She stared at it, exhaustion momentarily numbing understanding. "Oh shit!' she gasped.

Reception. She was in range! She sat down and, with trembling fingers, punched in one, one, one.

She watched the animated picture show that it was ringing. She placed it back over her ear. Ringing. Ringing. Why didn't they answer! Where were the bastards?

"Good evening," a precise female voice vibrated in her right ear. "Please state which emergency service you require."

Bree froze, then mumbled something incoherent.

The person on the other end must have thought she couldn't speak for some reason. "Don't hang up," the voice continued.

"Help us, please!" Bree finally blurted.

"I can help but you'll need to tell me who and where you are."

"Bree. Bree Ashworth. We're from the aeroplane that crashed on the way to Palmerston North. I'm calling on a mobile phone."

"Bree, this is Gwen. I can hear you clearly so just relax. Where are you calling from?"

Bree could hear a keyboard being tapped. "The mountains," she sobbed. "No, I've got it wrong. Ranges! We're on a cliff face under thick forest. Ray's caught in a slip. He needs emergency help."

"You're doing well, Bree," Gwen said. "Just explain everything. We'll get a trace on you and send out an emergency helicopter. Palmerston North Emergency Services have just indicated they are patched in and, as soon as we get a grid reference, we'll be on our way. First of all ..."

Gwen's soft voice continued and Bree stopped trembling. Tears rolled down her cheeks but she regained some composure. She told what had happened, what the terrain looked like and spoke to two other people before Gwen came back on the air with more encouraging words.

"We have a trace, Bree. The rescue helicopter has just left Palmerston North. You should hear it in about twenty minutes. If you have some clothing to wave..."

"Go to Ray first. I'm okay."

"We'll get you all, Bree. It's quite a large helicopter."

"Oh, thank God." Bree couldn't stop her chin trembling as her voice turned to sobs. She glanced up and saw the distant hilltops bathed in sunshine. Somehow, they seemed so friendly. She reached out, found Pattie beside her and just held the dog in her arms. My God, she'd done it. Ray and Jenny would be safe!

Bree wiped her eyes, hugged the dog and gazed around. She was in the middle of a pile of loose debris but a little above her there was a grass knob where a couple of trees grew. One was the bushy type they'd walked through all day and the other was a tall multi-branched palm tree that Ray had talked about when they were back at the hut. It had the unique name of cabbage tree.

Her thoughts went from the cabbage tree back to her friends. She stared down but could not see them in the deepening shadows. "Come on, Pattie, we'll go up to that knob and you can relax. A big machine is flying in to rescue us all." She laughed at her effort to explain things to a dog.

The outcrop provided a little shelter but a breeze had risen. Bree shivered. Her thin clothes offered no warmth and now that she'd stopped moving, a chill crept through her body. Her ribs began to throb. Bree grimaced. Other parts of her body hurt, too. Her face, arms and leg tops burned and there was a distinct line between the white skin beneath her blouse and the bright red skin over the rest of her body. Her legs and arms were scratched and she knew the blisters on her feet had enlarged. But that didn't matter. Help was on its way and that more than compensated for a few physical ailments.

As the blue sky turned to purple, Pattie cocked her ears up and whined. Suddenly, Bree saw flashing navigation lights and heard a thump of beating rotors. A black dot materialized between the lights, the noise became louder...and there it was. A helicopter was heading up the valley!

"Oh my God!" Bree screamed. She climbed to the outer edge of the knob and waved frantically.

The craft slowed, hovered and turned towards her. "Get Ray first!" she screamed, then realized her words were useless. She clung to a branch and just stared.

A chirping ring made her jump in fright until she realized it was the mobile phone. "Hello," she gasped.

"Bree?"

"Yes!"

"My name's Grant. I'm the pilot of the rescue chopper. We can see you and your friends. Are you okay?"

"Yes, fine." Bee shouted above the engine noise coming through the speaker and from above her. "I've got Ray's dog with me."

"No problem. Just stay where you are while we manoeuvre in beside you. A crewman will drop in and help. Just wait for him. Okay!"

The purple, green and white helicopter with *Square Edge Rescue* painted along the fuselage hovered in. Dust blew everywhere. Bree grabbed Pattie and watched as a man in an orange life jacket descended from the craft.

"Hi," he shouted. "I'm Tom. I believe you'd like a lift?"

Bree didn't know whether to laugh or cry so merely nodded.

Tom was beside her. "We've got a stretcher coming down," he said. "It won't take long."

Minutes later, Bree found herself swinging upwards with Pattie strapped in beside her. Wind tore the dog's hair, as the tree-tops disappeared. Arms reached out, a man grinned at her, shouted something she couldn't comprehend above the engine roar and guided them in. Tom was brought up, the door shut and the helicopter moved forward.

Tom wouldn't let her climb out of the stretcher. "Just relax, Bree," he said and guided an amazingly placid Pattie to a lead attached to the wall. "There you are, doggy," he said. "I'm in no doubt you've been a great help."

"Thank you," Bree sobbed.

"Part of the service." The pilot's voice came back. "I'm Grant. We spoke on the phone a few moments ago. You've met Tom and the doc, James Langton?"

Bree turned to the third man. "I'm sorry, Doctor Langton," she said. "I never knew you were a doctor."

"Welcome to New Zealand," James replied in a casual manner, "And where in England are you from, Bree?"

"London."

"I think I've heard of the place," the doctor said. There was a distinct twinkle in his eyes. "So let's have a look at you..."

Bree nodded but her gaze searched through the side windows. The slip dipped away and only the distant ranges and sky remained in sight. She noticed a sole star twinkle above the hills. Perhaps it was a satellite. The helicopter changed direction and the cliff face appeared again. She gasped. There were Jenny and Ray. She could see hair blowing across their faces. Jenny was holding Ray's arm with one hand and waving with the other.

CHAPTER ELEVEN

The Square Edge Rescue helicopter hovered over the pair and one of the first sights Jenny saw was Bree leaning out the open doorway.

"Hi," she mouthed but couldn't be heard above the engine noise.

A crewmember was lowered and smiled at them. "Hi," he said. "Tom's my name. Bree's given me your life's history." After a quick check to see that she was okay, he switched his attention to Ray. "You've a bit of a weighty problem there, Ray, but don't worry. We'll get Jenny up to the chopper then bring Grant and the jaws down."

"Jaws?" Jenny screwed her nose up.

"Jaws of Life. We usually use it to get victims out of mangled cars. It'll lift that boulder off Ray." Tom pointed to the harness he'd just taken off. "Now if you just slip this on, Jenny, and sit down on that rope thingie we'll have you aboard in no time."

Jenny nodded and a moment later she was hoisted up to the helicopter. A man helped her inside and out of the harness. He attached a machine that looked a little like a gigantic pair of hydraulic scissors to the winch and lowered it down to Tom.

"You look as sunburnt as Bree," he said. "I'll check you out after we've freed Ray if that's okay."

"Sure," Jenny replied. She made her way over next to Bree who greeted her with a hug. Not to be outdone, Pattie had to leap up to the extent of her lead and gave Jenny a sloppy lick.

"That's James, the doctor," Bree shouted over the roar of the rotors. "How's Ray?"

"Much the same," Jenny replied. "My God, were we glad to see you guys though."

"Jesus," the pilot called back. "Another Pom."

"That's Grant," Bree laughed. "He's a bit hard to understand but not bad for a local."

"Hi, Grant," Jenny shouted. "Thanks for the lift."

*

Down on the surface Ray was introduced to James, who immediately began an examination, asked questions and brought out a hypodermic needle. "This will relax you and dull the pain, Ray," he said. "I don't want to deaden it completely, though, as we'll need you to warn us if you are hurting when we begin to lift you out."

"Okay," Ray said.

"So who did the major digging?" Tom called. "The girls or the dog?"

"All of them. They did one hell of a good job, you know."

More gear was lowered from the helicopter and Tom slid the closed arms of the jaws in beside Ray, adjusted some controls and attached ropes and a net to the far side of the boulder. He glanced at the doctor.

"Ray should be okay," James said. "Just take it slowly."

As the machine expanded, the boulder lifted but tilted to one side. Ray gritted his teeth as pain shot through his body. Tom stopped the machine and placed a metal frame in the gap. He lowered the jaws so the boulder rested on the frame and carried the machine around to the other side where the boulder rested on the branch. Here he repeated the manoeuvre, inserted another frame and again glanced at the doctor.

"It's off your chest, Ray," James said. "You're lucky the branch left you some space. Don't move though. We're going to place two cross frames in and lift the right side. With luck the boulder will roll off to your left."

"Don't worry," Tom added. "These frames can hold the weight of an ten tonne truck without buckling."

Ray smiled and glanced up. All he could see was Bree's face staring down. God, she was attractive in that dirty green blouse, with her blonde hair blowing in the downdraft. She caught his eye and waved.

"We wouldn't dare hurt you with Bree watching," James said. "We never had school principals like her when I went to school. Most were males, overweight and over fifty."

"They were," Ray whispered. He felt lethargic as the drugs began to work but it was Bree above him that kept his courage up.

Everything worked as planned. The boulder rumbled a little and rolled sideways off the frame so there was now only debris around his legs to remove. The two men worked with care and precision with smaller tools and a vacuum device that sucked the chalky dust up.

Ray's legs appeared. The right one was misshapen and obviously broken but the other appeared normal. James immediately moved to examine him.

"I think your ribs are bruised rather than broken, Ray," he said. "There may be internal bruising but there appears to be no bleeding. I'll put a blow up clamp around your broken leg to support it and we'll get you aboard. How are you feeling?"

"Not too bad," Ray replied. His eyes became heavy but he was determined to stay awake if only to thank Bree.

James grinned at Tom. "Can you signal Grant to move away before that infernal downdraft blows us off the slip?"

*

"We're moving away so our downdraft won't hinder them," Grant shouted. "James is going to strap Ray in the stretcher. We'll return and lift him aboard."

The engine noise increased and the helicopter moved slowly away from the cliff face. Bree had a safety belt on but still stepped back as they swung around and began a slow circular flight. She gazed out and was sure she could see the lonely knob of trees below.

"That's where they picked me up," she shouted at Jenny.

"It was quite a climb," Jenny replied. "How'd you know the mobile would work there?"

"I didn't," Bree replied. "I was heading for the top."

"But you wouldn't have made it," Jenny said. "It's a sheer cliff. Look!"

Bree did. The area above the knob was far steeper than she realized from the surface. "I would have tried," she said in a far away voice. "There's no way I would have left you two there on the slip."

"Rational thinking or sheer pride?" Jenny asked.

"Sheer pride," Bree responded. "That or sheer foolishness, I'm not sure which."

"Guts," Jenny said and smiled.

*

The return was almost an anti-climax as they hovered over those still on the surface. James came up first and guided in the stretcher with Ray aboard.

"Hi, Bree," Ray said in a soft voice. He reached out for her hand but she was already there. She grabbed both his hands, gazed into his eyes, bent forward and kissed him on the lips. "My grandfather used to say that if a kiss received was not returned it would blow away in the wind to be lost forever. I didn't want your kiss to be lost."

"Bree," Ray said as he squeezed her hands. "I do believe you are a romantic."

She flushed and pulled back. "I'm just glad you had no serious injuries, that's all."

"Of course," Ray said. He winked at Jenny over Bree's shoulder.

Tom arrived, shut the door and moved up beside Grant. "Next stop Palmerston North Hospital," he said.

"So what injuries does Ray have?" Bree asked the doctor.

"He has a broken fibula in his right leg and some bruised ribs," James replied. "I want to examine you both more thoroughly when we get back. You all managed to get a right good sunburn."

"Yeah," Jenny interrupted. "Everyone else back home will have frostbite and we'll have the best tan in years."

*

It was dark when the helicopter landed at the floodlit heliport in the hospital grounds. Bree and Jenny were surprised to find themselves surrounded by reporters. At least one television camera homed in on them.

"The authorities reported that your aeroplane crashed above a waterfall in the ranges and was carried over. It was thought there were no survivors. Tell us, Mrs. Ashworth, how did you survive?" a woman asked as she held a microphone in Bree's face.

"We crashed above the falls," Bree replied. "The pilot was killed on impact but we were unhurt. Later, Ray Barnett found us..."

Other questions were thrown at the pair until James stepped forward. "Please, ladies and gentlemen," he said. "As you can see our survivors are exhausted and need urgent medical help." He bundled them into a waiting ambulance for the two hundred-metre journey across the car park to the Accident and Emergency Entrance.

"But what about Pattie?" Bree said as she noticed their mournful companion being held back from the ambulance by Tom.

"We'll look after her," Tom called and nodded towards an adjacent hanger. "I'll tie her up out of the night air and find her something to munch. Come and get her after your check-up."

"She'll be fine," Ray said. "I doubt if you two will be admitted, so it shouldn't be for long."

But it was. The trio were taken into a private room away from the reporters and asked to wait. James had just begun to examine Bree's wound when a nurse came up and spoke to him.

"Damn," he said and turned to his patient. "There's been a multi-car pileup on the main highway. I have to fly out in the helicopter." He grinned. "It's going to be another busy night, I think."

"But what about Ray?" Bree said.

"We have two surgeons on duty and they're both doing emergency operations. Ray is next on their waiting list. One of the nurses will admit him and take him up to a ward."

"And Jenny and I?"

"Your injuries won't require you to be admitted."

Bree frowned. "Of course."

"Is there a problem?"

"You could say that," Jenny said. "We've lost our luggage, passports, credit cards ...everything! "

James nodded. "We have a social worker I can call."

"No," Bree said. "I have all my credit card numbers, aeroplane ticket, and traveller cheques numbers recorded on an email I sent to myself before we left home. Tomorrow I can access it, so we should be okay for tonight. We'll just wait here."

"Right then," the doctor said. "But I must be off." He smiled and left the room.

"They're taking me upstairs in a few moments," Ray mumbled. "One of the surgeons is just finishing off his operation so should be with me in an hour or so."

"An hour!"

Ray laughed. "That's not too long, really."

"You can stay with Ray for a while," Jenny said. "I'll go out and see how Pattie is getting on. "See you soon."

She disappeared out the door but was back in less than ten minutes looking quite upset.

"Ray," she gasped. "Pattie's gone. I went back to the hanger. The helicopter's left and the place is deserted. Her leash is there but nothing else. I looked everywhere..." She bit on her bottom lip. "I'm sorry, Ray. I should have stayed with her."

"Oh my," Bree muttered. She looked at Ray but didn't expect to see the cheerful look on his face.

"Don't worry," he said. "She's probably gone home."

"Home!" Bree replied.

"I have a house only about a kilometre away. We often walked around these streets."

"But you said you lived in Auckland," Bree said.

"Oh, I did," Ray replied. "Sorry, I should have told you. The district office of the department I work for is based here. I bought a little house a while back." He told them where a spare key was hidden and laughed. "I was going to suggest you stay there. What motel would admit you vagabonds anyhow. Filthy clothes and no money."

"Ray, we can't." Bree said. "We can go to the motel we're booked into. There's still two nights to run."

"And leave poor Pattie cold and lonely outside an empty house?" Ray shrugged. "Mind you, she has a kennel out the back so I guess she'll survive."

"Ray!" Bree retorted. "You're teasing..."

"So, you'll baby-sit Pattie until I get discharged?"

"Of course she will," Jenny retorted. "But are you sure that's where Pattie's gone."

"If she's not waiting outside the hospital main doors, that's where she'll be." Ray reached in his pocket again, took out some money and a business card. "My address is on it," he said. "Here's forty bucks. Get a taxi and perhaps you could go to the supermarket and get a few supplies. I didn't think I'd be back so soon, so there's no fresh food at home."

Bree listened while gave other instructions. "Oh, Ray," she finally said. "You've done so much for us. I'm not used to someone being so kind. I..."

"Bree," Ray interrupted. "Shut up and go."

Bree nodded, bent over and kissed him. "Come on, Jenny," she said. "Let's go and find Pattie."

"Bye, Ray," Jenny said. "I'll come back if we don't find Pattie."

"Make it in the morning," Ray laughed. "Oh yes, I've got my car at home. My car key's on that ring. You can borrow my car to get around town, if you like."

"And if we just rip you off and disappear?" Bree said.

"Then I'm a poor judge of character and it'll serve me right."

CHAPTER TWELVE

46A Langston Avenue was only a few blocks from the hospital. The taxi driver drove down a driveway between two colonial style houses and stopped by a modern townhouse. As he turned in, an outdoor light came on to show a small but well-cared for front lawn, an attached double garage and polished front door.

Bree stared at Jenny with apprehension in her eyes. She paid the driver and watched as he reversed out and they were alone... for about twenty seconds.

There was a woof and Pattie came bounding around from the rear of the garage.

"Oh my God!" Jenny exclaimed as the Labrador jumped up and placed front paws on her tummy. "So you did come home? I thought I'd lost you forever."

Pattie ran over to Bree for a similar welcome, then dashed down the drive. "Ray's still at the hospital, Pattie," Bree called. "He'll be home tomorrow. Tomorrow! Understand."

Pattie, as usual, seemed to comprehend the situation, for her tail began wagging and she followed the pair up to the door. The second key Bree tried fitted and the little group walked in. Jenny managed to find a light switch and turned the interior lights on. Bree saw an open plan kitchen and living area. The room was modern and, apart from a slight musty smell from being shut up, looked like a home.

Followed by both Jenny and Pattie, she strolled around the room. It looked like Ray, somehow. Three wall paintings depicted outdoor scenes and the furniture was comfortable but unpretentious. Opposite the kitchen area was a computer, and a wall cabinet with glass shelves holding the usual odds and ends people put in such places. She stopped and took a photo frame off the cabinet. It showed a slightly younger Ray beside a woman with short dark hair, slightly chubby build and happy smile. The next photograph showed the head and shoulders of the same woman. In this one the smile was still there but the face had become thin and lined. The woman had aged twenty years between the two images, but Bree knew from, what Ray had said, that in reality, it was half that time.

"His wife?" Jenny whispered.

"I guess," Bree said. She placed the photographs back and went to pull curtains across the large windows that dominated the far wall. There was a tiny alcove she hadn't noticed and, at the end, another door.

"Probably goes to the garage," Jenny said and pushed it open.

When she walked in the lights came on automatically to reveal a conservatory. Though not big, the long room was encircled in glass. Three steps led down to a cobblestone path that twisted between two stone walls that held an indoor garden. Everywhere were plants, ferns, flowers, creepers and moss. The garden had the look of being recently planted but the design was such that already the place gave the atmosphere of being out in a forest. Taller plants hugged the outer space, then smaller flowering shrubs and at the front, flowers and ground hugging creeper. There was a slight sound of running water and Bree noticed an intricate system of black pipes with fine mists of spray fanning out.

"Look at this," Jenny said as she stepped along the conservatory.

Bree joined Jenny and her eyes lit up in delight. A kidney shaped fishpond twisted out from behind miniature shrubbery. But it was more than that. The stone wall became a miniature street. There was a stone bridge, several English styled cottages and models all to the same scale. Tiny figures, animals and vehicles filled the street. One stone building had a working waterwheel beside it. The whole model circled half the goldfish pond but a clear space beyond showed that work on it was unfinished.

"Ray must have added the conservatory after he bought the place. This had to have taken days and days to create. It's beautiful."

"But lonely," Jenny said.

Bree looked at her companion. "You sense it, too?"

"Imagine having all this with nobody to show it to?"

"He probably has lots of horticulturists who visit."

"So that's why he took the job up in the ranges?"

"I know," Bree said. "This conservatory reflects him doesn't it?"

"Like you," Jenny said. "Conscientious and dedicated, except he deals with plants instead of kids." She laughed. "Plants don't cheek you back or have irate parents to complain about missing shoes."

Bree chuckled. "Okay," she said and opened a second door in the middle of the one wall that wasn't glass. This led to the garage with a small Japanese car parked on the near side. The far space was empty but showed where a second vehicle usually parked. Like the house and conservatory, the garage was tidy with a workbench across the end and shelves along two walls. Most shelves were filled with horticultural items such as containers of potting mix, trays, clay containers and garden tools.

Another door led outside into the back yard. This still looked undeveloped but the lawn was cut short and a wooden kennel stood beside the garage.

"Your home, Pattie?" Bree said to the dog that had accompanied them the whole time. "So this is where you came back to from the hospital."

Pattie yelped, ran inside her kennel, and rushed out again with a well-chewed bone in her mouth.

"Okay, I've got the message," Jenny said with a chuckle. "You're hungry. Come on, girl. Ray must have left something inside for you."

*

The journey to the supermarket was an experience in itself. Newly washed, but still wearing their stained clothes, the pair walked out to the car. Pattie jumped in and sat expectantly on the back seat.

"You drive and I'll navigate," Bree said to Jenny. "I found a street map in the glove box."

"Sure," Jenny said confidently.

The next problem was a small matter of automatic drive. She'd only driven a manual back home and found after several attempts that she could only turn the key when one foot was on the brake pedal. Finally, they roared down the drive at far too great a speed, swung out on the empty road and screeched to a jarring halt.

"I thought the brake was a clutch," Jenny said with a little less confidence.

She found the drive position, turned onto the road and headed for the intersection. Suddenly, another car appeared. Lights dazzled them and a horn blared.

"Jenny," screamed Bree. "You forgot to turn the headlights on."

"Shit!" Jenny cursed and found the switch just as the other car careened by.

The corner was a major road with vehicles everywhere and huge overhead lights making everything as light as day.

"Turn right," Bree said as she gazed at the city map on her knees. "Go straight down here to the traffic lights. The supermarket is on the left just past the lights."

"Yeah! Yeah!" Jenny muttered.

They made it to Woolworths Supermarket, spent most of Ray's forty dollars and headed back. After they pulled into the garage, the automatic doors shut. Jenny wiped sweaty palms on her blouse and grinned.

"That was fun," she said until she caught Bree's eyes. "Yeah, okay. It was a bit scary but we've got food now. God, I'm hungry and my sunburn stings like hell."

They had just walked into the kitchen when the telephone rang. Bree glanced at Jenny and answered it.

"Can I speak to Mrs. Bree Ashworth, please?" a female voice said.

Bree frowned. "Speaking," she replied.

"This is Charge Nurse Deborah Richmond from Palmerston North Public Hospital speaking. You are a relation of Mr. Ray Barnett, I believe?"

"A friend," Bree replied.

"Oh, I see," the nurse replied. "One moment, please."

"It's the hospital," Bree said to Jenny.

The charge nurse came back on line. "Normally we'd only speak to a close relation but Ray has listed your name as the person he wanted contacted. He has just been taken into surgery."

"For his leg?"

"I am afraid it is more serious than that, Mrs. Ashworth. He has internal bleeding that has to be stopped."

Bree felt the colour drain from her face. "I'll come straight over."

"You're welcome, of course, but it will be at least two hours before you'll be able to see him or get a progress report."

Bree thanked the nurse and hung up. "Something's wrong," she said. "I'm going back to the hospital."

"Not without me," Jenny said.

They left the lights on with Pattie inside and arrived at the hospital within five minutes. However, they were not allowed beyond the Accident and Emergency waiting room. After half an hour, Bree was tired of thumbing through the inevitable magazines and began watching the television suspended in a corner. The movie that she hadn't really watched came to a close and the station switched to a late news broadcast.

"Look," Jenny gasped as the woman news anchor spoke.

"Further to our earlier bulletins about last weekend's plane crash in the Ruahine Ranges north of Palmerston North, it has been confirmed that the two English tourists, Mrs. Bree Ashworth and Ms. Jenny Dench, both from London, England survived. Jane Reddington reports from Palmerston North hospital. What is the latest news, Jane?"

"Oh my," Bree whispered as the picture switched to show their arrival in the helicopter. Of course, the reporter was the woman who shoved a microphone at her. The views of herself made her shudder. She never realized how scruffy and tired she looked.

"There's more," Jenny hissed. "We've never seen this."

The view switched to a rescue crew beside the wrecked aeroplane. The video shots showed the covered body of the pilot being carried away and placed in a helicopter. Bree stared, fascinated by the flooded stream and the water pounding over the waterfall behind. The camera turned and zoomed in on the raging fall while the reporter's voice added a commentary. "To survive a plane crash in these conditions is unusual, but to also walk away after being pounded over the falls you are now viewing is a miracle."

"That's not true," Jenny cut in but Bree waved her quiet as the scene switched back to the hospital doors they'd walked through a few moments earlier. Jane Reddington came back on air in what looked like a live broadcast.

"One of the women is having an emergency operation at this very moment but we are unable to verify who it is...."

"They got that wrong, too," Jenny interrupted.

"Oh well," Bree said with a shrug. "It doesn't matter." She was more concerned about Ray.

*

The news snippet though was of high viewer interest. Air crashes always piqued viewer interest but to survive tumbling over a flooded waterfall added doubly to that. The BBC World Service included it in their world news broadcasts an hour later. This was midnight, New Zealand time and eleven in the morning in the United Kingdom. By noon, the BBC home service and independent radio and television networks picked up the same report. After all, these were local English women who had survived a terrible crash in a far off land. It became the hot news of the hour.

An independent London radio station supplemented the news with a background item about Bree at Sunset Grove Primary School and had an interview with Deputy Headteacher Patricia McCarthy. They also rebroadcast the earlier item taken when Bree was attacked in Jenny's classroom. Even in sophisticated London, the pair became a topic of conversation for thousands of citizens over the next few hours before some other crisis took over.

*

The Accident and Emergency room filled with people from all walks of life. Three intoxicated youths covered in grime and blood staggered in. They were swearing and cursing until a security guard told them to either sit down or get out; a young woman in a dressing gown carried a tiny baby in her arms and was taken straight through to a cubical, and victims from some accident were wheeled through.

"They've probably been brought in by the helicopter," Jenny said.

This was confirmed when a tired James Langton walked in. He saw the pair, smiled and walked across to sit beside them. "Still here?" he said

"Ray's having an emergency operation," Bree said. "Internal injuries."

"Yeah," Jenny added. "They won't let us go any further and they tell us nothing."

James nodded and stood up. "I'll see what I can do," he said and caught Bree's eyes. "Don't worry. Ray's injuries are not life threatening. His pulse was strong and he's a healthy guy."

He disappeared and within two minutes a nurse arrived and walked straight up to them

"Bree Ashworth?" she asked.

"Yes."

"I'm Charge Nurse Debbie Richmond who spoke to you on the phone. If you'll follow me I'll take you up to the surgical recovery room. Ray should be coming out of the anaesthetic shortly." She frowned. "Normally only next of kin are allowed to see patients this early after an operation but Doctor Langton cleared you both."

"Good old James," Jenny said and raised an eyebrow when the nurse frowned. "Did I say something wrong?"

"No. Doctor Langton is the hospital's senior medical officer, that's all. He doesn't usually deal with A and E but we've had a rash of illnesses with the resident doctors."

"Nothing like the top to get some action," Jenny retorted. She grinned and gave Bree a dig on the arm when the charge nurse flushed.

In contrast to the waiting room, the surgical floor was a symbol of silent efficiency. The security guard outside the elevator nodded at Debbie Richmond but Bree noticed he checked a clipboard as they walked by. They were in a spotless corridor that had that distinct hospital aroma of cleaning fluid and medical supplies. After moving through two side corridors, they arrived at a small room with one hospital bed inside.

There, with a plastered leg in a sling held up by pulleys and counterweights, and a satchel of fluid dangling from a frame, was Ray.

"We set his broken leg at the same time as his operation," Debbie explained. "Ray may be disorientated when he awakes. I'll leave you but just press that button by his bed if you need assistance. A nurse will come straight away." She gave an expression as if it had better not happen, smiled slightly and disappeared.

"I think James stirred everyone up," Jenny said. "That head nurse reminded me of you when you're mad with a staff member."

"Thanks," Bree retorted. She walked across beside Ray; saw he was still asleep and glanced back at Jenny. "He looks pale," she muttered and stood with her fingers twitching.

"Sit down, Bree," Jenny whispered. "I've never seen you look so nervous."

Bree looked up. "I'm acting irrationally aren't I?" she said.

"No. It's the opposite, Bree. Why hold your emotions under a shell? There's nobody here except Ray and me. He's asleep and I won't tell."

"Oh, Jenny," Bree replied. Tears appeared in her eyes. "I'm all mixed up inside. God, I've known Ray only a couple of days but..." She took a handkerchief out, wiped her eyes and looked back at the man on the bed.

"So?" Jenny replied. "Time makes no difference. It's what happens during that time that is important."

"But nothing much has."

"Everything has, Bree. Clutch and embrace it while you can for it may never return."

"What mightn't?" Bree retorted.

Jenny said nothing but just smiled and squeezed Bree's hands with her own.

*

Ray dreamed he was in a room. A woman was bending over his bed, smiling at him. He knew the smile but didn't recognize the blonde hair and enormous blue eyes. It was a beautiful face, one filled with empathy, and he thought he should know the person. But it was merely a dream. He knew nobody so beautiful. Perhaps it was an angel. But shouldn't an angel be dressed in a long flowing silver gown? And why did she speak with an English accent?

He smiled and slipped back into a foggy cloud of nothingness.

His next conscious thought was of a warm hand holding his. He opened his eyes and saw the blue eyes again. There was the woman of his dreams, but he wasn't dreaming. She was real. She was there and he knew her.

"Hi, Bree," he whispered. "It was nice of you to come back. Did you find Pattie?"

*

"My God, I thought I'd never get you away from there," Jenny said as they drove home almost two hours later. She hit the remote to open the garage door and drove the car the last few metres inside.

Bree opened the passenger door and up bounded a very wet, dirty and smelly Pattie.

"Damn," Bree said. "Where have you been, Pattie?" She looked at Jenny. "The door to the conservatory?"

"Could be!"

They ran though the connecting door and just stared. The lights were on. The far end path by the pond was saturated with puddles everywhere. Across from this was a box of compost all gouged out as if Pattie had been rolling in it. Small clumps of compost mixed with the puddles to cover half the cobblestones in mud.

"Oh, Pattie," Jenny scolded. "You are a naughty girl, you know."

Pattie looked up and wagged her tail slowly as if she was uncertain how to react.

"Okay, young lady," Bree said. "We'll clean it up tomorrow but you're going to have a bath or be put out to your kennel."

She found a tin tub in the laundry that appeared to be for the purpose, filled it with warm soapy water and ordered Pattie in. It worked but both she and Jenny ended up as wet as the dog, and the mud seemed to transfer across, too. She towel-dried the dog and glanced up.

"Do you know what the time is?" Jenny asked.

"About one."

"Three fifteen."

"Oh my. I might just have another shower. I never knew looking after a dog was so much trouble." She turned to Pattie. "You stay off my bed after I make it up, too."

"You'd rather have Ray in it with you."

Bree turned. "Jenny, just shut up. Can't you think of anything else?"

CHAPTER THIRTEEN

Bree spent all of the next day at the hospital while Jenny did everything else. She went on to the Internet and found both their personal sites where they had recorded copies of their documents. Next, she rang the United Kingdom High Commission. The receptionists there said they could issue them with temporary passports but they would need to visit the omission office in Wellington in person to confirm their identity. Their credit cards were more of a problem, for by the time replacements arrived from their banks in London, they'd be home again. Luckily, both she and Bree had travellers' cheques that could be replaced locally when they produced the serial numbers.

"Right, Pattie," Jenny said after she returned from the hospital to find the dog looking left out of everything. "You can come with me downtown, we'll get some money and go shopping." She found a little notebook and jotted items down as she spoke. "First of all we both need clothes, backpacks to put them in, more food..." She stopped and stared at the ceiling. "Of course...our travel insurance. I forgot. All of this will be covered. Now if I find the local agent..."

Ten minutes later, she was off with Pattie sitting beside her. She had no idea whether local laws allowed dogs to travel in the front seat but it didn't really worry her. The first bank she walked into directed her onto a second where her traveller's cheques were verified and new ones issued. She could change her own for local currency but Bree needed to sign personally for her ones. The woman behind the counter was friendly and helpful and even found the name of the company that would handle her travel insurance claim.

An hour later, she had visited several quite large stores and bought clothes for them both. Perhaps Bree's tastes were more conservative than her own was but they were a similar size so she bought what she liked before moving onto something for Bree.

"She'll need a dress suit," she muttered to herself but after checking out the prices decided modern slacks and a couple of blouses would have to do. She giggled and found some clothes she was sure Bree wouldn't like but Ray would.

Afterwards, she returned to the car to find Pattie fast asleep across the back seat, so she went to find a coffee bar. It was hot, almost thirty degrees. She'd have to think more in metric. Everything in New Zealand was metric. Oh well! Half an hour later she returned to the car to find Pattie sitting on the front seat waiting.

"God, it's hot, girl," she said. "Let's find somewhere cool where you can walk."

They reached a river on the edge of town with a walkway along the bank. Dogs and people seemed to be everywhere. Pattie ran around while Jenny found a shady bench to sit on and read the morning paper she'd bought.

"Damn," she muttered.

Their story was splashed all over the front page with a coloured photograph of her and Bree standing beside Ray's stretcher just after they climbed out from the helicopter. She read the article and found it was far more accurate than the television news. On page three, a diagram showed how their aeroplane crashed above the falls and even suggested the pilot was killed then not after the wreckage was carried on over the falls. Arrows were superimposed on a map to show their journey to Taylor's Mistake Hut and onto the slip face where their rescue took place.

Pattie returned, stuck her chin on Jenny's lap and gazed up with round eyes.

"Okay, girl, we go walking." Jenny said. "Afterwards, you can wait while I go to the supermarket for some more food, then it's home for us both."

She stood and followed Pattie along the path.

*

In the surgical recovery ward at the hospital, Ray woke to find Bree still sitting beside the bed. "So what happened to the conference?" he said.

"I missed it," Bree replied. "Everyone's gone home."

"When are you going back to England?"

"We have another week. Originally, Jenny and I were going to visit the South Island but now..." She stopped. "I suppose we still could."

"And why are you hesitant?" Ray replied.

"You," Bree gulped. "I don't want to leave and never see you again."

"Why?" the whispered question followed.

Bree stood and turned away. She was about to move further when Ray reached out, seized her wrist and pulled her in.

"Ray!" Bree protested but he was too powerful. She almost crashed across his bandaged stomach but responded when he kissed her. The kiss became passionate until Bree wriggled and pulled away. "Not here, Ray," she said. "It's not right."

"Why?"

"I've known you only a few days, I'm an overseas visitor and I'm married. Is that good enough for you?"

"No," Ray said and grabbed her wrist again.

Bree turned with tears in her eyes. Ray grimaced and let her go.

"It's happening too quickly, Ray. You're lonely. I'm lonely. Lonely people make mistakes."

"True," Ray said. "So I'm acting like a spotty skinned adolescent?"

"I didn't say that."

Ray seized both her hands but just held them. "Will you do something for me, Bree?" he asked.

"Possibly. What is it, Ray?"

"Leave me. Go for a long walk, two hours or more. Talk to Jenny; get your passport and money sorted out. If you decide to go south and finish your holidays, there is a commercial kennel you can place Pattie in. I've used them before. Their name is written at the front of my telephone book." He caught a tear that rolled down her cheek.

"And if I come back?"

"It will be because you want to come, not because you feel sorry for me." He let her hands go. "If you decide to leave, do it in the morning, not a week from now. Understand?"

"I think so," Bree replied. "Take care, Ray." She stood, straightened her crumpled green blouse, and walked out.

Ray watched the empty doorway long after Bree was out of sight. "Bugger," he muttered. "I stuffed that up well and truly."

Charge Nurse Richmond slipped in from the other side of a privacy screen. "She's a pleasant woman, Ray," she said. "I have a feeling she is more than just appreciative about being rescued."

"And what would you have done if you were me, Debbie?"

"I'm not a male, the ball is in her court now but I reckon she'll be back before ten tonight." She grinned. "Probably right at the end of visiting hours."

"Interesting," Ray whispered. "A woman's mind is the strangest thing. I thought she'd be back within those two hours or not at all."

"No, she'll wait, perhaps even until the morning but she'll be back." The nurse frowned. "I hope you're genuine though, Ray. I think she deserves that."

"I am," Ray whispered.

*

The main roads of Palmerston North were built in a grid and stretched away to the distant sky. Beyond, another twenty-five kilometres away, was the ocean. In the opposite direction the distant ranges appeared as a cardboard cut-out against the cloudless sky. It was hot, and the heat reflected up from the footpath, so it was almost uncomfortable to walk upon. Bree didn't want to look at the ranges, so headed west towards the centre of the city.

Her mind played 'what if' as she walked. What would have happened if Ray had not found them above the wrecked aeroplane? Would they still be there, weak with hunger and exposure or would the official search team have found them? What would she now be thinking? What if her relationship with Colin hadn't broken down? There were questions by the score but no answers.

In almost a trance, Bree continued to walk. She crossed a main road at traffic lights and continued walking. A large, grassy park with a row of shady trees appeared across the road. Bree stepped out without checking for traffic.

The screech of brakes jolted her senses and she stepped back just in time, waited while a line of vehicles drove by, then walked over to the park. The grass smelled of the country and felt soft beneath her shoes. She reached the trees and glanced around. There was nobody around. She sat down and leaned against a tree. If she shut her eyes and ignored the traffic noise, she could be back in the bush. Perhaps this was what helped to make up her mind.

Bree stood and glanced at her watch. The two hours Ray suggested had gone. She clamped her lips tight and headed back. Five minutes later, she heard a toot and a small car pulled to the curb in front. A dog stared out the rear window.

"My God, Bree," Jenny yelled when Bree opened the passenger door. "I've been driving in circles for half an hour looking for you. Have you come to your senses yet?"

"What do you know about anything?" Bree said without attempting to climb into the car.

"Bree," Jenny snapped. "Get in, will you!"

Bree did but stared out the front window without even talking.

"Moody damn lot, both of you," Jenny said as she moved the car into the traffic.

"Both of us?"

"I went back to the hospital and Ray was like a bear with a sore head. I had to drag everything out of him."

Bree turned and gazed at her friend. "Thanks, Jenny," she whispered. "I'm lucky to have a friend like you."

"Yeah, I know. We're going home and you can put on the flash clothes I bought you. Then you can go and put Ray out of his misery. Right."

"You bought me some clothes?"

"Of course. You look positively revolting in those tacky things. You could give your hair a good brush, too."

"Oh, Jenny," Bree replied. "You're the limit." She smiled, turned and rubbed Pattie's ears. "Hi, girl,' she said. "Sorry I ignored you."

Somehow the long busy road looked more friendly now and the distant ranges positively inviting.

*

After Jenny left, there had been visitors all afternoon, but they were acquaintances from work that Ray had not known long. A departmental head arrived and told him his contract would be extended into the next year, and the surgeon said his operation was successful but he would not return to work for a while. His leg was taken from the sling and a nurse helped him into a chair beside the bed. She adjusted a pair of crutches to fit his long frame and asked if there was anything else she could do.

"I'd like some shaving gear, please." Ray replied.

The afternoon became evening and he became more despondent. The crutches were awkward and there was nowhere to walk anyway. He sat back in bed and grinned slightly when Debbie returned on duty and came to take his blood pressure and administer some medicine.

"What, no beard?" she said. "You'd better be careful or that young English woman won't recognize you when she returns."

"If she returns," Ray muttered.

"She will," the charge nurse said with a confidence Ray didn't feel.

*

"Hello, Ray," said a soft voice. "I brought you some fruit."

Ray jerked awake and stared.

Bree was dressed in a modern sleeveless frock that only partly covered the cleavage of her breasts. Her hair shone and her lips had just a touch of pink lipstick. Two tiny birds bounced from golden chain earrings. There was a whiff of fragrance in the air.

"My God, Bree, you look wonderful," Ray whispered.

"Not cheap? Jenny bought the clothes and insisted I wear them. I'm usually more practical."

"Come here," Ray said.

Ray crushed Bree into his chest until it hurt but absorbed the feeling of a warm sensuous body next to his. His body reacted instantly but he did not care whether she noticed or not.

"You shaved your beard off," Bree whispered. She rubbed her lips across his cheek and kissed him again. "Did you have to?"

"No, but I don't need it any more."

"And your leg," Bree said after they had unravelled and she stood back. "How's the cast?"

"Okay," Ray said and caught her eyes again. "You're beautiful, Bree. Even with the sunburn, I..." He gulped. "I'm not very good at saying what I feel."

"You're doing okay, Ray. So, where do you want the fruit?"

"And your decision?"

"I'm here, Ray. Doesn't this answer your question?" She held her right hand out and Ray noticed a small circle of white skin where she'd removed a wedding ring. "I should have done it ages ago but had no real reason until now."

"And your South Island trip?"

"Cancelled," Bree whispered. "Oh, I tried to persuade Jenny to go but she's staying, too. I hope you don't mind."

"Me? Mind?" Ray laughed. "No, Bree, I don't mind. We need someone to entertain Pattie, don't we?"

He reached up again and tucked his arms around her. She buried her head in his chest and they both hung on, deep in thought but satisfied with the decisions made.

CHAPTER FOURTEEN

Bree woke from a deep sleep. Someone was shaking her. She opened her eyes to find Jenny standing in front of her with a towel wrapped around her wet body

"Get up," Jenny whispered. "There's a car in the drive and someone's rattling the side door."

Bree glanced at the bedside clock and saw it was only a little after seven in the morning.

"Well, get up," Jenny prodded. "I can't do anything with nothing on."

Bree scrambled up, pulled a jersey over her pyjamas, tiptoed to the closed curtains and peeped through a gap. A modern, blue car was parked in the driveway.

"Why hasn't Pattie barked?" she asked. "God, she even barks when someone walks up the neighbour's drive."

Jenny shrugged. "I haven't seen her."

"Okay, I'll go and check but you'd better get dressed."

With thumping heart, Bree walked through to the kitchen and stopped in horror. The outside door was open. Someone was in the house! She moved silently across the room with senses on full alert and saw that the conservatory room was also open.

"If anyone is there, come out," she called in a loud, controlled voice that, she hoped, did not convey the tremor she felt.

Pattie ran out with her tail wagging.

"Pattie!" Bree said in relief. "Who let you in the conservatory, girl?"

"I did," a loud, icy female voice said.

Bree jumped in fright and glanced up. A plump, middle-aged woman stood in the conservatory doorway with an angry expression across her face.

"Who are you and why have you just walked into our house?" Bree demanded.

"Oh, I see," the woman replied, her voice quieter but hostile. "You're one of those English women Ray rescued. So, you're sponging off his kind nature and getting free board and lodgings, are you?"

Bree's own anger rose. "Yes, I am Bree Ashworth. Ray gave me and Jenny permission to stay here, but who, Madam, are you and why have you come in without even the courtesy of a knock?"

"Ray sent us a key, not that it is any business of yours."

"Come now, Emily, you can show some courtesy towards Ray's guests," a quiet male voice said.

Bree jumped in fright for the second time in as many minutes. She swung around to see a grey-headed man standing behind her. For a second, panic gripped as her retreat was blocked. The man, though, was smiling and had a hand extended.

"From all the reports, we have you to thank for helping Ray. I'm Ken Preston and this is my good wife, Emily." His hand clasped Bree's in a strong shake. "Please forgive her. She wasn't expecting anyone to be here." He chuckled and patted the dog "You must have made an impression on Pattie. She never told us you were here."

"Do you know Ray?" Bree asked.

"I'm sorry," Ken said. "We're Ray's in-laws. His wife, Maxie was our daughter."

Bree flushed. "Of course," she said. "I should have realized. Ray speaks highly of you both." She turned to the woman. "I'm sorry, Mrs. Preston. Ray didn't tell us you were coming."

"He didn't know," Emily replied in a warmer voice. "We drove all night from Auckland when we heard he was seriously ill in hospital."

"Ray's fine. He broke his leg and had an operation to stop internal bleeding but nothing is serious."

"Thank God," Emily replied. "We were camping at a remote beach and never heard a thing until we came home last night and there it all was on the television." She swallowed and appeared almost tearful. "I never expected to see another woman in Ray's home. I'm sorry if I reacted badly."

Bree nodded and was glad that Jenny chose that moment to walk in. "Jenny," she said. "This is Ray's mother and father-in-law, Ken and Emily Preston."

"Pleased to meet you, Jenny," Ken boomed and shook the astounded young woman's hand. "We apologize for frightening you but we had no idea you were in the house." He grinned. "Mind you, we should have guessed when Pattie met us in the kitchen. Ray would never leave her here by herself."

"Ray did say we could stay," Jenny said defensively.

"And why not?" Ken said.

Bree saw him give his wife a slight frown as she half opened her mouth. Ken Preston seemed friendly but his wife still looked frosty. "You must both be tired," Bree said. "How would you like to freshen up? I'll get us all some breakfast."

"That's great," Ken hesitated. "We'll look for a motel later. We had intended to stay here but with you both here..."

"No! Stay," Bree replied. She mentally kicked herself and thought of the cliché she'd quoted to Jenny the night before about putting her brain in gear first. She caught Jenny's ever so slightly raised eyebrows.

"Okay, we will," Ken responded. "Come on, Emily, we'll get the bags."

"If you say so, Ken," Emily replied and followed her husband out.

"So what else could I do?" Bree whispered.

"Hell, I don't know. Ken's okay but she's an old bat. Probably thinks you're going to steal her son-in-law away from her."

"Oh, that's silly."

"Why? They are still grieving their daughter's death, that's obvious, and the thought that Ray could be attracted to someone else doesn't go down too well."

"So say nothing," Bree said. "Anyhow, it's really up to Ray isn't it?"

Jenny nodded but could say no more as Ken staggered back in carrying two large, old-fashioned suitcases. "What room, Bree?" he said warmly.

"Jenny and I are using the first bedroom on the left. Otherwise..." Her voice tailed off.

"Okay," Ken said and disappeared.

Emily returned and helped with breakfast and was chatting away with Jenny when Bree slipped away to get dressed. Just as breakfast was about to be served, Jenny walked to the door. She stared, expressionless, at Bree and muttered something about getting some milk from the corner dairy and disappeared. Bree frowned. They had plenty of milk.

*

Jenny roared Ray's car into the hospital car park and headed indoors. Ignoring everyone, she walked to the elevator and headed up to Ray's ward. Nobody stopped her, and she walked in to find he was having breakfast.

"Jenny," Ray said in surprise. "What's wrong?"

"Your in-laws showed up." Jenny sat on the end of the bed, helped herself to a piece of Ray's toast and explained what happened.

"They're good sorts," Ray said when Jenny finished. "Emily's still getting over Maxie's death, that's all."

"No, it isn't," Jenny protested. "She's got it in for Bree. If it wasn't for Ken, I reckon she would have practically ordered us out of your house." She sniffed. "They've moved in, too, and I wouldn't be surprised if Bree decides to move out."

"Okay, Jenny," Ray said. "I admit Emily can be like that. I'll see what I can do. Who knows you came here?"

"Nobody. I said I was going to get some milk."

"Then you'd better buy some, hadn't you?"

"Sure," Jenny said. "Oh, Ray..."

"Yes?"

"I'm glad you and Bree are...well, you know. You're just what she needs."

"Thanks, Jenny," Ray smiled. "It's true everything's changed quickly but I guess this happens sometimes."

"Yeah, like Romeo and Juliet," Jenny said. "But I must go. Don't tell Bree I came." She squeezed Ray's arm and disappeared as quickly as she arrived.

*

Ray was deep in thought as he sipped his half-cold coffee. He knew he should appreciate Ken and Emily's arrival but why did they have to come now? Oh well, he'd have to think of some discrete way to show Emily he needed to move on in life and not just survive on memories. He grinned. Maybe instead of pretending Bree was just a casual friend, he should openly show his true feelings. His mother-in-law might stop trying to defend Maxie's memory. Perhaps he could add even more to the story...

However, there was no way to tell Bree of his plans because Ken and Emily arrived first. Everything went fine until the conversation turned to the English tourists.

"She's a good looking woman," Ken said with a twinkle in his eye.

"Which one?" Ray tried to remain casual

"Bree. The other girl is just that, a mere kid. Now, if I was your age..."

"Ken!" cut in Emily. She turned to Ray. "She's taken advantage of your good nature, Ray. She probably earns twice your salary and is getting free board. You know Jenny drives your car everywhere. I bet she doesn't bother to fill it with petrol, though."

"Don't you like Bree?" Ray said.

"Well, I hardly know her," Emily muttered "But after a week I doubt if you do either. I hope there's nothing more than friendship...."

"Why?" Ray's voice had an edge to it and he ignored Ken's quizzical look.

"Oh, Ray, she's from England. What could you have in common? Married, too. I know the sort; they come to a country like ours looking for a good time and don't care if they affect other people. Afterwards, they go home and continue their normal lives."

"That's where you're wrong, Emily," Ray said. "It is true Bree and I are, shall I say, more than friends."

"Didn't I tell you, Ken?" Emily interrupted. "One week and she's already played on poor Ray's emotions. I've a good mind to..."

"It's not a week. I've known Bree since August last year," Ray lied.

"How?" Emily blurted.

"I met her at that native forests conference in Auckland and again when I had that holiday in Queensland last November."

"And the plane crash?"

"She was flying down to visit me. When I heard of the crash I joined the rescue crews and found her." Ray never blinked under his mother-in-law's intense gaze.

"I see," she finally said. "Why didn't you tell us earlier?"

"For the very reason I almost never told you today, Emily. It wasn't that long after Maxie's death. How would you have reacted?"

"That's true, Emily," Ken cut in.

"I loved Maxie," Ray said. "Bree, nor anyone else, can never change that but I can't just live my life in the past, can I?"

Emily nodded. "She does seem to be a sophisticated young woman. I can see she suffered a lot as a result of the accident. Do you love her, Ray?"

Ray nodded and reached out for Emily's hand. "That doesn't mean I love Maxie's memory any less." Oh hell, there were tears in her eyes.

"Of course not, Ray, but what about me and Ken?"

"You know I have no parents, Emily. You have been my parents from even before Maxie's illness. That will never change. I will always need your love and support. That will never change. I just hope you can include Bree now."

"She's in many ways like Maxie," Ken said. "I can see why Ray is attracted to her."

"You would," Emily retorted.

Ray glanced up and saw that Bree and Jenny had arrived. He slid off the bed and hobbled towards Bree. Without forewarning, he swept her in his arms and deposited an affectionate kiss on her lips.

She stiffened and was about to pull away when Ray kissed her again, hoping that she would follow his lead.

"I was telling Emily and Ken about how we met at the conference in Auckland last August," he said. He used a little finger to tickle Bree's palm and felt her squeeze back.

"The conference?" Bree stuttered. "It's a while ago..."

"Yes, over four months now." Ray laughed. "You know, they thought we'd only met last week."

"Did they?" Bree's laugh sounded forced but perhaps he was the only person to notice. "I told you we shouldn't keep it a big secret."

"Oh Bree," Emily said. "I'm sorry if I was so cold. Ray's like a son to us and all we want is for him is to be happy. As I said to Ken on the trip down from Auckland, one can't live on memories can one?"

Ray noticed Bree's eyes that said, '*You've got some explaining to do here, buster*.' However, in a controlled voice she was quite diplomatic.

"I should have told you before, Emily but... you know," she said.

Ray grinned.

*

"Oh, my God," Jenny laughed the following morning back in the ward with Ray and Bree. "What a couple of con artists you two are."

"Well, it worked, didn't it?" Ray replied.

"Sure did," Jenny replied. "Emily and Ken couldn't be more helpful. Ken insisted on taking us to one of the top restaurants in town last night and wouldn't let us pay a penny." She chuckled. "Mind you, Emily gave him the evil dagger when he picked up the tab."

"She's not too bad," Ray said.

"You could have warned me, though," Bree cut in. "I was all prepared to act like a platonic friend when you crushed me with that kiss, then came up with that conference bit. I almost blew that."

"But you didn't," Ray replied. "You caught on quickly."

"Yeah, her experience at being a headteacher," Jenny said.

"Anyhow, we maintained the peace and they're going back to Auckland in a couple of days," Ray said. "There's no harm done."

*

The tall man in a business suit waited impatiently at the inquiry counter until the receptionist glanced up.

"Could you tell me where to find one of your patients, please?" he said in a pronounced English accent.

"The English tourists involved in the aeroplane crash?"

"That's correct."

"Wait one moment." There was a click of keyboard keys and the woman looked up. "Mrs. Ashworth was treated as an outpatient and discharged."

"So, where can I find her?"

"We are only permitted to disclose a patient's contact address to their designated next of kin or a close relation."

"I understand," the man replied. "I'm her husband, Colin Ashworth."

The receptionist frowned. "You are not listed on the file, Mr. Ashworth."

"That's understandable. Bree isn't expecting me. When I heard about the accident I flew straight here."

The receptionist glanced up. "We will need identification before information is released."

Colin impatiently took a passport from an inside pocket and handed it across the counter. "Now, will you tell me where my wife is?" he said.

"Her contact address is care of the *Chancellor Motor Lodge* in Fitzherbert Avenue."

Colin sighed. "I've been there. They said that she never arrived and the booking was cancelled."

The woman gave a superficial smile. "My only suggestion is that you contact Mr. Ray Barnett. He was the gentleman who arrived with Mrs. Ashworth and Miss Jenny Dench."

"And how do I do that?" Colin's voice was now caustic.

The woman frowned and tapped more information into her computer. "I'm sorry," she said. "All I can give you is Mr. Barnett's local address." She wrote it on a slip of paper and handed it across to Colin. "It's only a few blocks from here. Turn right out of the hospital car park and right again at the traffic lights. It'll be the third or fourth street on your right. You'll be able to see the signpost."

"Thank you," Colin replied and walked out into the afternoon sun.

He drove his rental vehicle up the drive of 46A Langton Avenue and glanced around. The place appeared deserted but he walked up and knocked on the door. A moment later, a middle-aged woman opened the door.

"Good afternoon," Colin said. "I am Colin Ashworth."

*

Perhaps Emily Preston had not heard Bree's surname for she made no connection between the visitor and her son-in-law's girlfriend. She stood and waited for the visitor to continue speaking.

"Is this the home of Ray Barnett?" Colin asked.

"Yes, but I'm afraid I'm the only one home at the moment. Can I take a message?"

"I'm looking for Bree, actually. Do you know her?"

"Bree!" Emily's eyes lit up. "Of course I know Bree. She's Ray's..." She waved her hand in the air as she tried to think of an appropriate word. "...Err, partner."

"I'm afraid I don't understand," Colin replied.

Emily frowned. With his accent, this fellow was certainly an Englishman, probably another of those reporters that were still annoying them. Mind you if he was English, perhaps he was from one of those big newspapers like the London Times. She hoped it wasn't one of the racy tabloids they also had over there.

"What do you young people call it?" she flustered when she noticed the man looked impatient. "Cohabiting...is that it? Oh, we never did it in our day. Of course, not every bride was a virgin but it wasn't like it is now."

Colin's face darkened. "I thought they were strangers," he almost spat.

For a second, Emily wondered why this man looked so annoyed, but he was a Pom, after all. They were a frosty lot at the best of times. "Oh, lordy no," she said. "They've been lovers for ages, a couple of years or more..." Emily smiled. Perhaps she had exaggerated a little but what the heck.

"Two years!" the man whispered.

"At least," she said. "They met at some conference somewhere. It might even have been back in England Ray did go overseas on a trip but I thought he never went beyond Australia." Emily began to enjoy being so helpful. "Apparently, they hit it off straight away Mr..." She stopped. "I'm sorry, I never picked up your surname."

"Call me Colin."

"Of course, Colin, but I'm afraid she's not in. Everyone including Ken, my husband, went for a drive out in the country. The car was full so I said I'd stay behind and just relax. We drove down from..."

Colin interrupted her before she could even tell him about her trip down. Young people were so impatient.

"Yes, yes," he said. "But, can you tell me any more about Bree and Ray?"

Emily smiled. "She's such an attractive young woman, principal of a primary school in one of those upmarket suburbs in London probably not far away from where you work...err...Colin. Far too young for such a position of responsibility, I sa, but..."

She rattled on with very little factual information but plenty of opinions and suggestions about Bree's lifestyle. When she finished the visitor thanked her and turned away. "Would you like to leave a message?" she asked.

"There's no message, thank you. I'll catch up with her another time," Colin said and drove away.

Emily shrugged. "Strange man," she muttered to herself and returned to the casserole she was preparing. Hopefully, it would be all cooked before the family arrived home.

*

Colin's rage was barely being contained as he drove across the city to his motel. How dare any wife of his have an affair and hide it for two years! He thought back. That was even before their marriage headed for the rocks and he began to screw Linda Rouke. Linda, that stupid cow was becoming a pain in the ass, too.

"The bitch," he snarled, not really sure which woman he was talking about. His mind switched back to Bree. If only that other bastard had...Colin slammed his fist down on the steering wheel in frustration.

He roared into the car park of the best motor lodge in town and headed for the bar. An hour later, he staggered back to his room with a bottle clutched in his hand. It was empty.

God, he needed company!

The telephone book had one well-fingered page. He glanced through the short list, tossed it away and turned to a local paper. In the middle of the classified ads was small photograph of a buxom girl.

Colin grinned and reached for the telephone.

A soft voice answered. "Brenda speaking. Can I be of assistance?"

"I need a companion," Colin said in a contrived calm voice. "Is that photo in your add one of you?"

"That's me, honey. And your name?"

"Colin."

"An Englishman. I just love Poms. Now, a massage starts at seventy five for an hour."

"Listen, girlie." Colin's voice almost showed anger. "I want two hours and I want it now."

"I see," the woman's voice became business like. "Two hundred but I take credit cards. You wear a condom and I don't go into kinky stuff. If you want that, I can refer you to a colleague. It'll cost you, though."

"No, you'll do," Colin replied and gave her the address. "Wear street clothes. Nothing exotic."

"Sure, Colin. I'll be with you in thirty minutes."

Three hours later, a badly beaten young woman tried to look dignified as she limped away from the motel. One eye was closed and already bruises were appearing on her cheeks. She wiped blood from her lips and grimaced in pain as she slid into her car and headed to the police station.

"Hello, Brenda," said the duty sergeant. "Someone go a bit too far this time?'"

"The bugger," she retorted. "I want him nailed and quartered."

The policeman sighed and reached for an official document. "Okay, Brenda," he said. "But shouldn't you go and see a doctor first?"

"That can wait," Brenda replied. "This guy is a maniac. He practically killed me." She lifted her head up. "Look at my throat."

Ugly red marks showed a distinct outline of fingers and a thumb.

"Where is he?"

"*The Swordsman Motor Lodge,* Unit Sixty-seven. The bugger will be asleep, I reckon. He reeked of spirits."

"Okay, I'll get a squad car there."

It took less than ten minutes before the police car screeched to a halt outside *The Swordsman Motor Lodge* and two officers made their way to Unit Sixty-seven. However, the door was open and a well-dressed man was wiping bloodstains off the bathroom wall.

"I'm the manager," he muttered. "If you're looking for the guy who hired this unit, he's just booked out. It was a funny time so I came and inspected the room." He sighed in disgust. "Look at the mess."

CHAPTER FIFTEEN

After threatening to discharge himself if he wasn't allowed out in the sunshine for a few hours, Ray sat in the front seat of his Toyota while Bree drove. Jenny, Ken and Pattie crowded in the back seat.

"Don't worry about leaving Emily behind," Ken said. "She doesn't like the beach much anyhow."

"But look at that sun," Jenny said. "Who's coming swimming when we get there?" She glanced at Ray. "Is it a good swimming beach?"

"Great, but keep your jandals on," Ray replied. "The sand will scald your feet in this weather."

"Jandals?" Bree asked.

"Those things on your feet."

"Oh, thongs." Bree said. "I thought you called them thongs."

"No, that's in Australia I think."

"Oh, Ray," Bree laughed. "I'll never get used to all your strange words."

They arrived at Himatangi Beach and Bree followed a line of cars onto the sand. Blue waves rolled ashore and hundreds of swimmers frolicked in the surf between two red and yellow flags.

"Keep between the flags," Ray warned. "There can be rips, so the surf patrol always picks the safest spot. Also, you could get hit by surf boards further along."

"I'm going in," Ken announced. "Jenny is I know but what about you, Bree?"

"I am,'" she replied. "It's different from Mount Maunganui but that surf looks so inviting."

"Yes, West Coast beaches are more exposed and have higher breakers," Ray said. "God, I wish I could go in."

"What about Pattie?" Jenny asked

Ray laughed. "She'll go crazy in the surf. She loves it."

And Pattie did. She ran in and out several times and shook water over the two young women, who were still dry. Next, she charged after Ken swimming out in the breakers. Bree found the water cool but, once wet, she loved the surf. Jenny kept with her and time slipped by.

Meanwhile up on the beach, Ray erected a massive sun umbrella and gathered up driftwood. He settled down with his back against a log and watched Bree. When everyone arrived back, exhausted but happy, Ray lit a fire and began to cook some sausages on sticks. They crackled and hissed as fat dripped on the naked flames. He wrapped a slice of bread around each cooked sausage, squeezed some tomato sauce on and handed one each to Bree and Jenny.

"None of those namby-pamby things you guys have," he said. "This is the real stuff."

Smoke curled up around them, and Bree had a coughing fit with tears rolling down her eyes. Ray grabbed her and fanned the smoke away. He kissed her cheek and laughed when she almost dropped the sausage.

"Well, it's hot," she protested.

"And if you aren't careful you're going to get sunburned again," Ray replied. "Here, wrap a towel over your shoulders."

Bree gazed into his eyes and smiled. She sat down and began to spread sun block over her skin. "I'm covered in sand, " she moaned.

"The sand brushes off when it's dry," Ray said.

So the summer afternoon rolled by and, all too soon, they headed back to Palmerston North where Bree escorted Ray back to his ward.

"So I won't see you tomorrow?" he asked after a passionate embrace.

"We'll be back," Bree replied. "It doesn't take all day to drive to Wellington. It's only about a hundred and forty kilometres away." She grimaced. "It's a nuisance having to personally uplift our duplicate passports but I know they need the security." She kissed Ray and returned to the others waiting in the car.

"Emily will have a flash meal waiting for us," Ken said. "I didn't tell Ray but I can't stick those burnt sausages covered in sand."

"What!" Jenny retorted. "I loved them." She pouted. "They were pure fat, though. My hips are already complaining."

They arrived home to the smell of the casserole; Emily fussed around and told them nothing important had happened while they were away.

*

Bree waved good-bye to the Prestons and Pattie as they reversed their car down the drive, turned and headed towards the corner. She noticed a square shaped Landcruiser parked across the road and thought for a second that it was somewhat out of place in the suburban street.

Jenny sat with a map on her knees and chatted. It was another hot morning and the city limits meant just that. Straight away, they were in the country with green fields stretching away in every direction. The ranges formed a boundary to the southeast and the plains stretched ahead to the coast they'd visited the day before. The two-lane highway was straight but narrow, with only light traffic coming in the opposite direction.

"You turn left ahead," Jenny directed ten minutes later. "Then it's over the river, a few bends and another long straight."

The road curled up over a massive stop bank, down into a flood plain over the Manawatu River and across the next stop bank. There were a couple of twists before they came to a small settlement. Bree slowed and pulled to the roadside when she noticed a country school with children playing in the playground.

"What a lovely setting," she said. "They've even got a swimming pool."

Jenny peered in the wing mirror. "That Land Rover has been behind us from before we turned off the other highway," she said. "It's still there."

"Probably a local farmer," Bree replied. "With so little traffic around it's just natural it is still with us."

"So why did it slow down and stop when we did?"

Bree shrugged and pulled back onto the road. The highway was now built higher than the surrounding land. Grass fields turned to an expanse of cultivated land with potatoes growing in rows. The road shoulder consisted of a narrow grass verge beside a deep drainage ditch. With no opposing traffic in sight Bree had to be careful to stay within the speed limit.

"Bree!" Jenny suddenly screamed in alarm. "That Land Rover! It's not slowing."

Bree glanced in the mirror. The Landcruiser was closing the distance between the two vehicles. If anything, it appeared to increase speed but did not pull out to pass.

Bree accelerated and their nimble little car pulled away. The road surface made the car vibrate and difficult to control. Her eye caught the speedometer that hovered around a hundred and twenty. Even in kilometres an hour that was too fast for the rolling surface. She slowed and Jenny screamed. The Landcruiser was so close only its front bumper and grill were visible.

"Go faster, it's right behind."

But it was too late.

The vehicle hit their back bumper with a shuddering crunch. Bree swung the steering wheel towards the centre of the road and accelerated rather than braked. This deft movement helped her remain in control.

"It's coming again!" Jenny yelled.

The Landcruiser had also braked and swung diagonally across the road in a cloud of blue tyre smoke. It straightened and accelerated towards them. The car was faster though and slowly pulled away.

"A bend." Jenny pointed to a sign ahead.

"I see it," Bree whispered.

It wasn't just a curve, but a ninety-degree turn, well sign-posted but still there. Bree braked and swung into it. Her driving skills proved to be successful for the car made it and headed along another straight section of road.

The pursuing vehicle had lost twenty or more metres before it accelerated back up behind them.

"Go!" Jenny screamed.

But Bree didn't. Her hands were covered in perspiration but her mind was on overdrive. If she accelerated, she might lose control. It was too much to hope that they could continue at this deadly speed. She never touched the brake but lifted her foot off the accelerator and the car slowed.

"Are you crazy?" her passenger howled.

"Look for a side road," Bree replied but there was no time for more conversation. The Landcruiser was right behind.

The driver's tactics also changed. The vehicle moved out to the opposing lane and moved up beside them. Bree glanced sideways and shrieked.

There, peering across the intervening space was Colin, her husband. She knew that dark look; those almost closed eyes and determined lips. He always appeared that way before he attacked her with a violence that she wouldn't talk about.

The panic disappeared as quickly as it arrived and was replaced by sheer determination to survive. "You won't kill us, Colin," she whispered and went on attack.

If the heavy vehicle sideswiped them they'd be pushed into the ditch. Braking probably wouldn't help and it was too late to accelerate so Bree did the only other thing possible. She swung the tiny car into the Landcruiser.

For a microsecond, Bree's eyes met those of her husband. The uncertainty was now his!

Steel screamed and buckled, sparks flew, the scenery spun and the car's passengers plunged forward to the extent of their seat belts. They dropped back behind the Landcruiser, spun around and stalled in the middle of the road.

The Landcruiser was not so fortunate. It headed across the road, Colin over-compensated, and his vehicle hit the grass verge, wobbled and bounced back on the road. Smoke howled from screaming brakes. The Landcruiser hit the grass on the near side; inside wheels lifted and the cab toppled.

Outside wheels spun and the centre of gravity was breached. A noise like thunder cut through the air as the Landcruiser skidded across the grass on its side and plummeted into the three metre deep ditch, that was really a drainage canal to take water away from adjacent swamp land.

The silence that followed was unnerving.

"Jenny," Bree cried. "Are you okay?"

"Fine, Bree," Jenny panted. "And you?"

"I'm not sure," Bree replied. She found reverse and backed the car off to the edge of the road.

Ahead there was no other vehicle, only black tire marks across the road and a massive gouge of bare soil where grass had been uprooted.

"It was Colin," Bree whispered. She hit the gas, swung out to avoid the Landcruiser tire marks and would have accelerated away to put space between her and the man who had violated her so much in the past.

Jenny, however, placed a hand on her shoulder. "You have to stop, Bree," she said in a loud but unexpected calm voice. "I doubt if he will be any condition to do anything to you."

Bree braked and pulled the car to the road shoulder. For a moment, she leaned over the steering wheel gasping and staring ahead.

"Are you all right?" Jenny asked.

Bree turned. "Of course I'm not bloody all right," she gasped. "That bastard... Oh hell." She opened the door, staggered out and vomited on the grass.

Jenny followed and tucked an arm around her shoulders. "Come on, Bree. You'll be fine. We're safe and it was your driving that did it."

Bree glanced up with lips quivering. "My husband tried to kill us, Jenny," she repeated. "The bastard. What have I ever done to him?"

"But he didn't, Bree. We survived. I'm going to tell Ray how you saved us."

"Come on," Bree said and climbed back into the car.

"Bree." Jenny pleaded. "We have to go back and see what happened. Stay here if you wish and I'll do it."

"I wasn't going anywhere," Bree whispered. She waited while Jenny went around and sat in the passenger seat and reversed back up the road to where only the wheels of the Landcruiser showed above the crumpled grass.

"Oh God!" Jenny gasped after they had made their way through the ripped and flattened grass. The Landcruiser was upside down in the dry ditch but there was no cab beneath, just tortured metal, broken glass and stream hissing up from a ruptured radiator. The smell of petrol and burning rubber whiffed through the air.

Bree stood, transfixed and watched while Jenny made her way down the slope and bent down to gaze through the gap that was once the driver's window. For a moment, she just stared before she turned and made her way on all fours back up the bank to Bree. Her face was ashen.

"Well?" Bree stuttered.

"I think he's dead, Bree. By the look of him I'd say his neck, and just about everything else in his upper body, was broken."

Bree nodded and stood shaking in her friend's arms. Tears rolled down her cheeks. That could have been them rather than Colin in that mangled wreck.

*

The following days after the accident were ones Bree wouldn't wish on her worst enemy and it was still not over. She had been summoned back to the police station and waited nervously for yet another interview. Even though Ray had tried to reassure her everything would turn out okay, she was not confident. She had already admitted she had recognized her husband as the driver of the other vehicle and had purposely turned her car into it. Back home, the authorities would be ruthless in a similar situation and now she had just been told an Inspector Cosgrove wanted to speak to her. This sounded ominous. Constables or sergeants had taken all the previous interviews.

A middle-aged man in blue uniform with pips on his sleeve walked out to meet her. "If you would come into my office, Mrs. Ashworth," he said in a soft voice and glanced up at the constable behind the counter. "Could you bring us both a cup of coffee please, Tami?"

"Yes, sir," the young woman replied and gave Bree a smile. Whether it was of pity or sympathy, Bree wasn't sure.

The inspector invited her to sit and opened a document. He read for a moment before looking up. "It has been a harrowing week, Mrs. Ashworth," he said.

"It has, Inspector Cosgrove."

"I see you are a primary school headteacher back in Hammersmith, London. You have done well."

"Thank you," Bree muttered. Her heart raced and she wished he'd get on with the grim truth.

However, the man smiled, thanked Tami who arrived with two coffees, and handed one to Bree. She thanked him, added milk and waited.

"We have a witness that confirms your statement that the Landcruiser driven by your husband was trying to ram your vehicle, Mrs.

Ashworth," the police inspector said. "We also believe your action in those last seconds before the accident was the only possible one."

Bree blew a sigh of relief and waited while the police officer continued.

"We further believe it wasn't an accident but a premeditated attempt by your husband to drive you off the road. However, since he was killed in the resulting collision, and no third party was involved, we have decided not to investigate the matter further. No charges will be laid against you. I wish to extend my deepest sympathy to you and your family."

"Thank you, inspector," Bree replied. She sucked on her lip. "...And the other matter?"

The police officer glanced up. "It is true your husband was wanted for questioning by us. A young woman laid a complaint of sexual assault against him."

"A prostitute?"

"I am not at liberty to say, Mrs. Ashworth."

Bree sighed. "It doesn't matter, Inspector Cosgrove. It's happened before."

"Will you need any assistance with the funeral arrangements?"

"No, thank you. The funeral director has been excellent. Colin's body will be cremated here in Palmerston North and his ashes returned home."

The inspector stood and shook Bree's hand. "It's been a tragic visit to our country, Mrs. Ashworth," he said. "First, the plane crash and now this accident."

Bree nodded, smiled at Tami who held the door open and walked out into the sunshine.

"So it was as I predicted?" Ray said after he'd kissed her.

Bree nodded. "Jenny's statement helped and apparently another witness saw everything. I guess it was that driver who stopped a few minutes after the explosion." She sighed. "There's only tomorrow's funeral service and we can put all this behind us."

"Did the police reveal anything new?" Ray asked.

"Not really. Colin had been in the country only two days and beat up a woman the night before. They found no motivation for his actions, so I guess we'll never know."

"It was jealousy," Jenny said. "He found out about you and Ray and was insanely jealous."

Bree glanced at her. "But who would have told him?"

"Who knows?" Jenny shrugged and dug Ray in the ribs. "Helps though, aye?'

"What do you mean?" Ray replied.

"Well, you aren't chasing a married woman and have to wait for her divorce now, do you? Here's only a grieving widow to look after."

"Jenny!" Bree gasped.

"Yeah, I know... shut up. But it's the truth, you know."

"And told with your usual finesse and charm." Ray chuckled. "Come on, ladies. I'll shout you both some lunch. That's the least I can do."

Bree smiled and followed as Ray swung his crutches out and headed for the nearby mall.

CHAPTER SIXTEEN

With Ray back home, the Prestons still there and the police inquiries over, Bree decided it didn't matter what other people's opinions were and she'd do what she wanted. She moved into Ray's bedroom to his delight, Jenny's approval and icy body language from Emily.

Ray grinned as she packed her new clothes in a dressing table drawer and turned to stare into his eyes. "All my life, I tried to help and please others and do you know what, Ray?"

"It's an impossible task?"

"Exactly. Take Emily for example. Once they go home, I'll probably never see her again. If she doesn't like me or what I do, what the hell." She pouted. "My mum was like her. I guess that's why it grates."

"I know," Ray replied. He tucked his arms around her and kissed her neck. "So, what happens when you do go home?"

Bree turned around. "I don't know," she whispered. "I have to go back, of course. I just told myself I couldn't care less about other people, but I do. There are all the wonderful people around me. I love you, Ray but I don't know why."

"Why try to diagnose everything? Just let it unfold..."

"Ray," Bree cut in. "Didn't you hear me? I said I loved you, more now than before Colin's death and you react by..."

Her words were cut off when Ray kissed her with a passion Bree didn't expect. She responded but struggled away, blinking tears. "Is that it, Ray?" she whispered. "Is it merely the sex?'"

"No," Ray said. "I love you, too, Bree." He grinned. "There you are, I said it. Now, how about having a shower with me?" He dragged her, protesting, through to the bathroom.

Bree never objected as he methodically removed her clothes and thrust her under the warm shower. She tipped hair shampoo over him and ducked under his arms. He caught her halfway across the bedroom and carried her to the bed. There, he made gentle, wild love with her. Afterwards, Bree realized the shower was still going so went into the cramped steamy cubical built for one. Ray followed and they made love once more.

"Oh my God," Bree whispered afterwards as she slipped into pyjamas and rubbed her hair with a towel. "You're the limit."

"What limits?" Ray chuckled.

Bree attempted to glower but merely managed a smile as she crawled between the crisp red sheets on their bed. "I'm going to sleep," she finally said.

*

The sun had just risen when the telephone rang. Ray was snoring so Bree reached across him, grabbed the instrument and answered it.

A sobbing, barely coherent voice filled her ears. "I wish to speak to Bree Ashworth, please," the voice gasped.

Thoughts whizzed through Bree's mind. The voice had a London accent. It was not, though, someone she recognized.

"This is Bree speaking," she said.

"Oh, Bree, this is Linda Rouke speaking. There's nobody else to turn to." Sobbing prevented words for several seconds before the voice continued. "It's Colin..."

Bree frowned. Of course, Linda would have heard of his death. She'd contacted relations back home and arranged for a funeral notice to go in London and Birmingham newspapers. One of her friends back home said she would contact Linda.

"I'm terribly sorry, Linda. It was a tragic accident..." she began.

"I want to come to his funeral," the other woman blurted out. "But I can't afford the air fare."

"I see," Bree replied. "Of course, you're welcome to come. We are going to bring his ashes home and have a memorial service in London, you know. It's what his mother wants. You could come to that."

"No, I need to come to his funeral. Oh, you don't understand..."

The woman was extremely distressed.

"So it is important that you are here?" Bree said after managing to calm Linda down.

"Yes."

"Do you have a joint account or money of your own?"

"A little of my own but not enough, "Linda replied. "Colin always handled the money. He gave me an allowance."

That sounded like the man. He always wanted to dominate.

"Okay, Linda. I'll get you the ticket and it can be paid for out of Colin's estate. There's not a lot of time, though. The funeral is the day after tomorrow. You only have about thirty-six hours."

"Oh, Bree, you'd do that?"

"Isn't that what you wanted?" Bree replied, her voice without emotion.

"Yes. It's just so terrible. I need to be with him one last time."

"Okay, Linda. Give me your telephone number and email address. I'll call back early tomorrow morning, your time." She hung up and found Ray's arms around her shoulders.

"The girlfriend?" he asked.

"She's devastated, Ray. What else could I do?"

"Bree, that's one reason I love you. It would have been so easy to say sweet things and hang up the phone but you didn't."

Bree grimaced. "And, given the circumstances, you would have?"

Ray smiled. "No, I'd have done the same," he replied. "If you give me your credit card number I'll go get her a ticket."

"Ray, it's five-fifteen in the morning."

"On the internet, my love," he said, kissed her and disappeared out the bedroom door.

*

The flight from Auckland arrived at Palmerston North Airport at one-thirty and the funeral was at four. Bree, Ray and Jenny waited in the small terminal as passengers walked in from the Air New Zealand aeroplane. It was another scorching day and most of the passengers were dressed in shorts or light clothes.

She recognized Linda at once and grasped Ray's hand. The woman wore light slacks and a loose blouse but it did not cover one obvious fact. She was pregnant.

"Oh shit," Jenny whispered. "No wonder she was distressed."

Bree swallowed and attempted to cover her utter surprise.

Linda looked blankly around the terminal. Her tired eyes lit up when she saw Bree walking towards her. She looked nervous but also relieved at the sight of someone to meet her.

"Linda," Bree said. "You look exhausted. I never realized you were..." Her voice trailed off. "Colin was the father?" she added.

"Yes," Linda replied. "I can't hide it, can I?"

"Nor should you," Bree replied.

Her mind was in turmoil. She thought of her own pregnancies. Neither had progressed as far as Linda was now but the last could have if, in one of his rages, her husband hadn't beaten her so badly she had lost the child. It would have been a little girl. She studied Linda. Sure, she looked exhausted but there were traces of abuse, too. Her bare arms showed bruises and Bree was sure there was a thin scar across Linda's cheek.

Jenny must have realized Bree's dilemma for she took over the conversation. "Hi, " she said. "I'm Jenny, Bree's travelling companion. She was going to come here with Colin but..." She gulped and flushed.

"I know," Linda replied. "Look, I'll stay at a motel tonight and return to Auckland tomorrow." She shook her head and wiped a hand over her eyes as if trying to clear her senses. "I had to come, though."

Bree cut in. "You will stay with us. I'm not going to leave you alone in a strange country." She turned to Ray. "Tell her she's welcome, Ray."

Ray introduced himself and supported Bree. "There's room at my place if you don't mind sharing a bedroom with Jenny." He smiled. "Come on, I'll get your bags. There's time for you to clean up and relax for a while. If you'd like to visit the funeral home, I'll take you but that'll have to be soon, I'm afraid. The undertaker will be taking the body out to the crematorium at three."

"Thank you," Linda replied. "I'm a little tired. Twenty-six hours on the flight across the world was a long time." She glanced across at Bree. "It feels all wrong, like a terrible dream. Even now, I can't really grasp what happened."

"Come on," Bree said. She put an arm around the Linda's quivering shoulders. "You're with friends now."

Linda blinked back tears "Am I?" she whispered. "Your husband's mistress, carrying his child, here for his funeral."

Bree swallowed. "There is no animosity, Linda. You didn't break us up. My marriage to Colin was over well before he met you."

Linda gave a tiny smile. "He wasn't an easy man to live with, was he?"

"No, but let's not dwell on that, now."

While they talked, Ray led them to where the passengers' luggage was circling around a conveyer belt. Linda pointed out a large pack, and Ray lifted it onto a trolley. The group walked out to the car, where Bree insisted Linda sit in the front. She walked around the car to where Jenny waited

"Did you see her bruised throat?" Jenny whispered.

"No," Bree admitted. "I saw her arms, though. Poor kid. I'm glad we're here to help her."

"Yeah," Jenny replied. "It takes two to tango, though, doesn't it?"

There was no time to reply but Bree caught Jenny's somewhat unsympathetic eyes. Linda was no angel but seeing the woman so heavily pregnant jolted her memories to what might have been. When she slipped into the back seat of the car, she caught Jenny's eyes. Nothing was said but Bree knew her friend understood.

*

The funeral was subdued; Linda cried continuously, Bree sobbed, Jenny shed a few sympathy tears and Ray looked glum. Emily and Ken insisted on coming and joined the family near the front of the tiny crowd. The rest of the mourners were strangers but some introduced themselves. Two were New Zealand representatives from the company Colin worked for and another two, police officers. Who the other dozen or so mourners were, Bree had no idea.

When the service was concluded she walked over to thank the funeral director. After the usual courtesy comments she remarked on the number of flowers around the coffin and also the memorial hymn sheet that had been distributed. It had a photo of her late husband on the cover.

"His mother couldn't be here but sent most of the flowers," the man said in a hushed voice that funeral directors usually cultivate. "She sent his photograph over as an email attachment and asked for it to be used. I tried to contact you about it this morning but you were out. I hope you didn't mind."

"Not at all," Bree replied. "Thank you. I appreciate your thoughtfulness."

"It's been a tragedy and I'm glad I could help." The man rubbed his nose. "Who was the young pregnant woman with you? I heard her English accent and noticed she was quite distressed. The deceased's sister or close relative?"

Bree's lips dropped. His smooth talk annoyed her. "Mr. Franwell, she is my late husband's mistress and it's his child she's carrying," she retorted and walked away.

Bree received another surprise before she reached the car where Ray, Jenny and Linda were waiting. Emily intercepted her halfway across the car park. She held the memorial sheet in her hand.

"Bree," she said in a voice as hushed as the funeral director's. "I didn't know or I would have told you."

Bree frowned. "Told me what, Emily?"

"Your late husband. I recognized his photograph. The day before the accident he came to Ray's house looking for you."

"What?" Bree's voice was loud.

Emily reddened. "I thought he was an English reporter. It wasn't until now that I... I'm sorry, Bree. I didn't know it was Colin."

"What did you say to him?" Bree hissed.

"Not a lot, just general stuff about Ray and you..."

"Ray and me?" Bree retorted. "What did you tell him about Ray and me?"

Emily's hand shook. "Only what you and Ray told me, how you met earlier, had that holiday together..."

"How long, Emily? How long did you say I'd known Ray?"

Emily shrugged. "A year or so. I may have said two years. Does it really matter?"

Bree gave an audible sigh. "No, Emily, it doesn't matter. It helps to explain something, that's all."

"Did I do wrong?"

Bree managed a smile. "No, Emily, you did nothing wrong. How could any of us have guessed Colin would turn up at this end of the world?"

Emily smiled and was about to say more when Ken appeared. "So what's all the big discussion?" he said.

"Colin called into our place that afternoon we went to the beach," Bree said. "Emily never realized who it was until she saw his photograph."

Ken stared at her. "Now that is a coincidence," he said but his expression showed he knew it wasn't one at all. He reached out and brushed her arm. "We're going home in the morning but there is something I want you to do, Bree," he said.

Bree nodded but said nothing.

"You're both invited to stay at our place before you leave New Zealand. It'll be an early morning flight out, won't it? Bring Ray, too."

Bree smiled. "Oh, Ken," she said. "I'll love to come," She turned to Emily, "And don't you worry about Colin. It makes no difference anyway, does it?"

Emily smiled. "No, it's poor Linda who has the burden now, I suppose." She shook her head in wonderment. "I'll never understand this present generation."

*

"God, it's hot," Linda exclaimed when they finally arrived back at Ray's place. "Coming from mid-winter to this is almost too much."

Bree glanced at her companion. She thought Linda had come through the traumatic afternoon well but it appeared the bubble of adrenaline had burst. Linda was hollow-eyed, with streaks of mascara dissolved in perspiration making her face gaunt. Her lips trembled and her hands shook.

"It's over now," Bree said with empathy in her tone. "Come inside, have a hot bath or shower and rest." She glanced at her watch. "It'll be the middle of the night in England now. You must be exhausted."

Linda managed a smile. "It's been the longest day in my life," she said. "Literally. I didn't know how you'd react but I never expected this kindness from someone I hardly know."

"Just by reputation," Bree cut in and immediately chastised herself for being blunt.

Linda, though, didn't appear concerned. "Colin gave the impression you were a cold, old maid of a school ma'am only interested in your work and little else." She wiped the perspiration off her brow. "You know the ex-wife syndrome. He wouldn't have said anything nice even if he felt it."

"I know," Bree said. "But what the hell, let's go inside and relax."

*

After a shower, Linda appeared more refreshed but still looked tired. She accepted Ray's offer of the bed in Jenny's room. Emily clucked around and, within moments, the mother-to-be was fast asleep. The others sat around the kitchen table and discussed the day's events. Linda's condition was the hot topic and Emily almost lectured the others on the declining morality in the twenty-first century.

Bree though, said nothing but sat looking melancholic. Ray slipped an arm around her. "Come on, my sweet. It's a beautiful evening. Let's go for a walk. I haven't shown you the park I take Pattie for a walk around, have I?" Ray chuckled. "My God, she's been tied up in her kennel all afternoon. She hates being left out there. I won't be a moment."

Bree walked down the drive but was soon meet by an excited tail-wagging dog that ran up, circled around, brushed her legs and darted back to Ray.

"Oh, Pattie," Bree laughed. "How could we forget about you?' She knelt down and tickled the dog's ears. "We're going to the park."

Pattie ran her nose in Bree's face, barked and tore ahead down the footpath, around the corner and out of sight.

"She'll be back," Ray said. "The park's only a block from the hospital. That's why I wasn't concerned when she disappeared after we first arrived. This is her home turf." He slipped his hand into hers. "She what's wrong? The funeral, Linda or her condition?"

"You noticed?" Bree replied.

"I noticed how kind you are to a woman barely able to cope, how tolerant you are with a well-meaning but gossipy middle-aged lady, and I love you for it all."

Bree squeezed his hand but her eyes watered.

"What is it, Bree?"

"Linda's pregnancy."

"I thought as much. It made you think of your own, am I right?"

Bree nodded.   "The last time, I was careful.   The doctor was excellent and everything went well... until... " She stopped and stared ahead at Pattie who had just reappeared. "Colin came home drunk and screamed how fat and ugly I was. I replied it was his child I was carrying and he..." She squeezed Ray's hand until her muscles hurt. "He attacked me. I fell and he kicked me...." Ray slipped his arm around Bree's shoulders as she continued. "I was rushed to hospital but my little girl was stillborn," she wept.

"So you noticed Linda's bruises, too?"

"He never changed, Ray. He was arrogant and violent and deserved to die. I hope the bastard rots in hell." Her voice was venomous. She glanced up. "But I feel so, so sorry for Linda. Colin had nothing, you know... financially, I mean. Oh, he was well off at one time. In fact he inherited quite a large amount when his father died a decade ago, but blew it all on stupid business attempts and hot tips on the share market. Gambling never helped, either." She patted Pattie with her free hand and glanced at Ray. "I think Linda tricked him into getting her pregnant; perhaps it was to keep him with her."

"And would it have worked?"

"No, he was never interested in children." Bree replied. "Perhaps one reason he came out here was to use me as an excuse to move on." She chuckled. "My God, it must have cut his ego to threads when he thought we'd been having an affair for two years."

"Two years!"

"Yeah, that's what Emily told him."

"When?" Ray said in amazement.

Bree glanced up. "Didn't she tell you?" Ray's expression showed he knew nothing so she told him everything.

"And one little white lie grew?" Ray laughed. "Emily always exaggerates."

"Yeah. Knowing Colin, he would have flown into a rage and decided on instant retribution."

"So we now know the motive."

"We do," Bree replied. "I'm fine but poor Linda..."

"But you aren't responsible for her," Ray said. "She's a grown woman, just one of millions who find themselves alone in the world with a baby due."

"She's barely older than Jenny."

"So? Jenny has her head screwed on. In fact, she's probably more mature than Linda."

"That's what I mean," Bree replied.

CHAPTER SEVENTEEN

Their last week in New Zealand went far too quickly. Bree insisted that Linda travel back with her and Jenny and had their tickets changed. Their own fares incurred an extra charge from the original bookings but Linda had paid the full price anyway so the transfer was made without difficulty.

Ray flew up to Auckland with them and everyone stayed with the Prestons. Now, they were at Auckland International Airport waiting for the final minutes before their departure.

Emily walked over to where Bree stood. "Bree," she said

"Yes, Emily?"

"All the best, my dear. I thought nobody could replace our Maxie in Ray's eyes but I was wrong. Do you have to return home so soon?"

"I'm afraid so," Bree replied. "My headteacher's job is waiting for me."

Emily twittered her fingers. "I mean permanently, Bree. You're the best thing that has happened to Ray. Come back to him if you can." She reached out, squeezed Bree's hand and walked away.

"I intend to," Bree murmured, the turned as Ray moved up beside her."Well, Ray," Bree said. "It's back to winter."

Ray nodded and leaned his crutches against a nearby wall. "Come here," he said.

They kissed with passion before Bree wriggled away and wiped her eyes. Ray swallowed and handed her a receipt. "Something for you from the duty free shop," he said. "You pick it up in the exit lounge." He squeezed her one last time, grabbed his crutches and stood back.

"Come on," Jenny said. She hugged Ray and urged Bree after Linda and the other passengers along the exit corridor.

At a right angle corner, Bree turned. Ray was still there. He smiled and blew a kiss. Bree waved, swallowed and headed out.

"Your gift," Jenny reminded and led Bree to the duty-free shop counter.

The gift was tiny but Bree gasped when she was finally aboard and pulled the wrapping away to discover a velvet jewellery box. She unclipped the clip and opened the box. Inside was a gold and diamond bracelet. The tiny card had a short message in Ray's handwriting.

Until we meet again. We both love you, Bree. Ray and Pattie.

"Oh my," Bree said and burst into tears.

"Shit," Jenny said. "That would have cost the mint."

"I can't take this," Bree sobbed. "Ray can't afford it."

It was Linda who replied. "And how do you propose giving it back, Bree?" she said. "Jump off the 747 as we taxi along the runway?" Bree glanced up and saw Linda also had moist eyes. "I wish someone cared as much for me as Ray loves you."

"Someone will one day, Linda," Bree whispered. "I'm sure of that."

CHAPTER EIGHTEEN

The third Wednesday in March was an even more than hectic time at Sunset Grove Primary School. It was the time of spring conferences; school closed at midday and throughout the afternoon and evening parents arrived at their allocated times to see the teachers. Jenny had just finished a particularly tough discussion with a parent who had the strange idea her son could do no wrong. The reason he was behind in math and reading was because Sunset Grove in general, and Miss Dench in particular, were not teaching the subject correctly.

Jenny sighed and glanced at her timetable. Oh thank God, she had a twenty-minute break before the next parent arrived. Her relief turned to a frown when there was a tap on the classroom door.

She placed the last child's records in the filing cabinet and tidied her desktop. "Come in," she called.

A young woman walked in carrying a baby wrapped up in a shawl.

"Hi, Jenny," she said. "One of the other teachers said you were free for a while."

"Linda!" Jenny cried. "My God, you look grand. And your baby!"

Linda beamed. "This is Casssandra, born only three weeks past."

Jenny smiled at the baby. "She's beautiful! What are you doing here in London? Have you seen Bree? Damn, why didn't you call or send a text message? It's been ages..."

"Questions, questions." Linda laughed. "I'll try and answer them."

"Can I hold Cassandra?" Jenny said.

"She's got wet napkins."

"God, I don't care," Jenny replied and cuddled the little girl in her arms before looking up at Linda. "Well?"

"I'm back permanently," Linda said. "Mum convinced me to come home." She screwed her nose up. "It's only for a while until I get settled. How's Bree? I haven't seen her yet."

"Fine," Jenny replied. "Works too hard, though."

"And Ray? Do they keep in touch?"

Jenny grinned. "Yeah. He rings her a couple of times a week and sends emails on the other days. They've got it bad."

"So what are they going to do?"

Jenny shrugged. "I've no idea. Bree's shut up on that one. Just mutters, 'We'll see' when I ask her." The pair chatted on until there was another knock and the next parent appeared.

"Am I early?" the woman asked.

Jenny glanced up. "No, come in Karen. I'm just talking to a friend." She turned back to Linda. "Bree's around. If you go downstairs you'll find her office across the hall. She'll be there somewhere."

"Sure," Linda replied. "That's if she's not too busy."

"She won't be."

*

The light on the console glowed to show the call was an internal one.

"Bree speaking," the headteacher said.

"Bree," Jenny couldn't keep the excitement out of her voice. "Linda's here with her baby. I've got another interview so I've sent her along to you."

Bree's heart leapt. "Linda here... in London? And..."

"Yeah, that's what I said. But must go. See you."

The telephone went dead and the intercom buzzed.

"A Ms. Rouke wishes to speak to you, Bree," said the office assistant. "She hasn't an appointment but insists it will be okay."

"Give me a moment then send her in, Anne," Bree replied.

She stood, straightened her skirt and walked over to the window. Her mind was awash with emotions. The baby. How would she handle that? She knew Linda planned to name the baby Cassandra Ashworth. And why not? Colin was the father. Still, Bree couldn't stop wondering about the small Ashworth she, herself, had lost. She wished Ray was here to support her. God, she missed him...

"Hi, Bree," said a quiet voice.

Bree turned and saw Linda holding the baby. Blue eyes stared out from a shawl.

Bree's heart melted. "My God, Linda," she whispered. "What a thrill it is to see you! And this must be Cassandra. She's gorgeous."

"You caught her at a good time. Wait until she's hungry. She'll howl the house down."

"Oh, Linda," Bree continued. "You look wonderful. I was just saying to Jenny the other day we should go and visit you, and here you are. Tell me, how is everything?"

Linda shrugged. "It's been difficult," she admitted. "Oh, I'm not too bad off. As you know, Colin left the house in Birmingham to me. By the time I sold the house and paid the mortgage there wasn't enough to buy here, hence my time at home with Mum. But how are you?"

Bree raised her eyebrows. "If it wasn't for Ray, it would have been as if I was never away. You know, you have exciting things happen and come back on a high, expecting everything to be different somehow." She shrugged. "But it wasn't. The school is still here with the ongoing hassles. I must admit Patricia, my deputy, did well those few days I had leave. She had all the records done and even solved a couple of ongoing problems I'd forgotten to deal with."

"So you could have stayed in New Zealand longer?"

Bree laughed. "Yes, nobody's irreplaceable are they?"

"But we are better off without some."

"Colin you mean?"

Linda nodded. "He wouldn't have stayed," she said. "Being a family man wasn't in his makeup. I clung to a fantasy that once our child was born he'd change." She sighed. "So, here I am back home with Mum and the new boyfriend."

"You've got a new boyfriend?"

"No, silly," Linda said. "Who wants someone with a newborn on her hips? My mother has a new boyfriend. Oh, he's pleasant enough sort of guy but I can't see myself staying with them too long."

*

Three weeks later, Linda moved into a small flat with Jenny. It was an arrangement that worked well for them both. Linda had companionship and an amazing amount of help with her baby, while Jenny came home after a hard day at work to find a warm and friendly atmosphere and, often as not, a meal simmering in the kitchen.

Bree immersed herself in schoolwork and arrived back home every night to find an email message from Ray waiting for her. His messages were long and detailed with information about his work and news about his conservatory plantings and Pattie's latest exploits. Every Saturday evening, Sunday afternoon in New Zealand, they'd talk on the telephone, two people still in love but separated by half a world.

Bree told Ray everything except one secret she shared with nobody. However, it was quickly coming to a point where her information would have to be disclosed.

CHAPTER NINETEEN

Ten days later, DS Robert Lueker phoned the school and asked if he could have an appointment to see Bree. "We've made some progress," he said. "And could Miss Dench be there as well?"

Bree frowned. "We'll be free at eleven," she said. "Jenny can be here but I'll need to ring Linda."

"Thank you," the detective said. "I thought it would be easier to meet at your school rather than my grubby little office. I'll see you at eleven."

At eleven, almost to the minute, Lueker walked in with DC Margaret Blackburn, the detective constable who interviewed Bree and Jenny after the classroom attack.

"Margaret's been assigned to help on the case," Lueker said.

"Which one?" Bree asked.

Lueker glanced up without even a hint of a smile. "We believe your late husband was behind the attacks and also that aeroplane crash in New Zealand."

"What!" Bree gasped. "Wasn't that an accident?"

DC Blackburn smiled at Bree. "Do you remember that we took skin and blood samples after your attack, Bree?" she said.

"Of course, but what has that to do with the aeroplane crash in New Zealand?"

"Initial investigations by the New Zealand Civil Aviation Authority found that a small explosive device had been attached to the Cessna's engine. They handed the matter on to the local police."

Jenny gasped.

"There's more," Lueker said. "They found some fingerprints on a section of the engine that survived the crash and the results were handed on to us."

"Why?" Bree asked.

"They belonged to the same man who was seen by witnesses hanging around the school on the day you were both attacked."

"What!" Bree gasped.

Lueker looked pleased with himself. "He's a local criminal known who goes by the name of Brad Selby." He glanced at Bree. "Have you heard the name before?"

"No."

"I have," Linda cut in. "Colin mentioned the name. I think he was a business partner."

"Oh he was more than that, Ms Rouke. Brad Selby is a thug who specializes in strong-arm tactics. He usually works alone but has connections with organised crime both here and across in Birmingham. We believe he was employed by your husband to have you killed, Mrs. Ashworth."

Bree stared in disbelief. "But why?"

DS Robert Lueker glanced up. "We were hoping you could help us with that question," he said.

Bree shook her head, but Linda chimed in.

"Money. Everything Colin did ultimately came down to that."

Bree looked at her, dazed. "Yes, you're right. At the end of our marriage I had it and he didn't."

"Was there anything else? Life insurance for example?"

"Oh my God," Bree whispered. "Of course. I had a life insurance policy from when I was a teenager. After our marriage, Colin persuaded me to increase its value to a fifty thousand pounds, which isn't really a lot. It was one of those endowment policies I'll receive when I turn sixty. The premiums weren't too bad so I agreed."

Lueker nodded. "Did it have any other clauses?"

Bree stared at him and paled slightly. "Yes," she added. "I remember we laughed about it at the time. In the case of a death by accident or unnatural causes there would be a pay out of a million pounds."

"So we now have motivation. If you became divorced he wouldn't be next of kin, so time, from his point of view, was running out."

"Colin was capable of that," Bree whispered.

"He needed money," Linda cut in. "Some great deal he was going to make millions from in Birmingham collapsed and he owed heaps. I think one of the banks was about to foreclose on him."

"So back to Selby," the detective said. "We think that after the attack here was thwarted, he followed you to New Zealand, Bree. Perhaps your late husband put him up to it. Anyway, he placed an explosive device on the aeroplane you were booked to travel on. A mechanic who worked on the aeroplane confirms that an Englishman came up and talked to him. Apparently, he convinced the chap he was aviation official. "

"But the guy was at our fancy dress," Jenny said. "I remember him."

"He's a professional, Miss Dench. I would say part of the contract was that killing Mrs. Ashworth had to look accidental. He deliberately used you as bait to attract Bree but also wanted it to appear that you were the primary object of the attack. He was just covering all the bases, so to speak."

"So he'd have killed us both?" Jenny whispered.

"Probably not," the detective replied. "You were probably better as a live witness to support the theory you were the main object of the attack."

Bree cut in. "But how did he know we were booked on an airline on the other side of the world. I changed our bookings after Jenny decided to come with me."

"Did you pay by credit card?" Lueker asked.

"Oh hell, I did. I've had the same card for years. Colin could have easily had the number."

"It wouldn't have been hard to contact the airline and find out what flights you were booked on."

"So where is he now?" Bree whispered.

"We arrested him at five this morning," the detective said.

Bree sighed. "Can you make any charges stick?"

"The evidence from both of you about the assault and attempted sexual violation should help prove any charges we make. The New Zealand authorities would also like him extradited to answer murder charges."

"But we're alive," Jenny said.

"The pilot isn't," DC Margaret Blackburn replied.

"Oh...of course."

"Are we safe from any associates of his continuing his dirty work?" Bree said.

"He worked alone. I think the local underworld would be glad to have him off their patch. He'd become a liability, you see."

Bree stared at the detective. "It makes me feel ill, Detective. Is human life so casual to these people?"

"I'm afraid so, Bree. You can be thankful you're still alive. We were investigating your late husband as well, you know. "

"No, I didn't," Bree replied, She glanced at Linda.

"I suspected but didn't want to know," the younger woman said softly.

*

After the police left, Bree leaned back in her chair and watched her two friends. "Oh, hell," she finally said. "I've been pretty naive all the way through."

"I don't think so," Jenny replied. "You were a victim, Bree. We were all victims, weren't we, Linda?"

Linda nodded. "But I ended up as a solo parent because of my stupidity."

"But would you go back?" Bree asked.

Linda shook her head. "No. Cassandra is my life now, Bree. I could never wish to be without her." She stood up. "Speaking of Cassandra, I must go. Mom's looking after her but she's hopeless with feeding and changing napkins. I'll catch you later, Jenny. Bye, Bree."

She left and Jenny turned to Bree. "There's something you aren't telling, isn't there?'"

Bree bit on her lip. "I have to tell you sometime so now's as good as any."

Jenny waited.

"It'll start to show soon," Bree blurted out. "I'm pregnant. "

Jenny grabbed a chair behind her and sat down. "Oh hell, that was something I never expected. Who's the father?"

"Jenny!"

"Okay, I'm thrilled but what does Ray think of it all?"

"I haven't told him."

"Why not?"

Bree sighed. "I love Ray, Jenny, but don't want him to feel committed because of my condition. If I tell him he'll be out here on the next aeroplane and I don't want that."

"Why?"

"He has his job, his lovely home, Pattie."

"But he wants you, Bree."

"Don't you tell him, Jenny," Bree warned. "Don't say a word to anyone."

"Of course I won't say a word," Jenny responded. "That's a promise."

*

Jenny kept her word not to 'say' a thing. However, that evening after Linda had gone to bed, she sent Ray an email.

Dear Daddy ... the message began.

CHAPTER TWENTY

Doctor Sandy Lynch was not only Bree's gynaecologist but also a personal friend.

"So we're in new territory now, Bree," she said after a very thorough examination.

"How so?"

"You've been pregnant longer than on any of your previous occasions."

Bree sucked on a bottom lip. "Superior genes and no physical violence," she muttered.

Sandy glanced up at Bree. "The ultra-sound results are through. I can tell you the child's gender, if you wish."

Bree stood without saying a sound and stared out the surgery window. Outside was a flowering shrub with several small birds flying around. In some ways, they reminded her of the fantails back in New Zealand.

"A pregnant pause..." Sandy remarked in a kind voice. "There is no need..."

"No," Bree replied. "I would like to know."

"She is a healthy little girl, Bree."

Bree sat and gripped the chair arm. "Oh my," she whispered.

"So don't you think it's time to tell Ray?"

"I guess."

"Bree, you're assuming things that may or may not be true but it is not your decision to make."

"I'm scared, Sandy. I need Ray to want me for what I am, not because I'm carrying his child. We live in different countries with different cultures. I have a career here and he has one back in New Zealand. Is it unfair to expect him to give up his way of life."

"Or you yours?"

Bree smiled. "I thought of that, too."

"So now is the time to discuss it with Ray and work everything out together. Isn't his input important?"

"Yes, extremely."

The doctor made a note in a notebook. "You can't hide your physical condition for much longer. Who else knows, Bree?"

"Everyone here," Bree replied. "I told the members of the Sunset Grove Governors at this week's monthly meeting and placed a formal announcement in this week's school newsletter."

"Any reaction?"

"Unexpected," Bree replied. "Everyone was thrilled, but their main concern was that I might leave. The governors want me to remain on as headteacher and ..." Bree sighed. "It's actually made things more difficult."

"You mean if there was a groundswell of indignation on a morality issue you could have resigned and had your options made for you."

"Something like that," Bree replied.

"So that makes it even more essential that you discuss everything with your child's father. If you procrastinate it will only become more difficult." The doctor fixed her gaze on Bree. "You should continue to have a healthy pregnancy, Bree. However, with your history of miscarriages, placing this stress on the situation will do far more harm than good, From a medical point of view I suggest you contact the father forthwith and tell him." Sandy smiled. "As a friend, I think your worries about Ray are without foundation. Just look at the bracelet you're wearing."

Bree nodded and fingered the bracelet on her wrist. "Okay, I will," she whispered.

*

Showers threatened as Bree walked home from the underground station. With only three months to go until her child's birth and the summer holiday arriving she could fly out to New Zealand and be with Ray. They could... Oh my, here she was again trying to make all the decisions herself. The first thing was to tell Ray and see what he wanted.

She walked up the steps into her home. It was the same, of course; silent and lonely. Using her foot, she slammed the door and headed in.

A noise caught her attention and a massive Golden Labrador bounded around along the hallway and straight up to her.

"Pattie," she cried as the dog leapt up at her, all sloppy tongue and wagging tail. "Pattie... but how can you be here?"

She grabbed the dog and hugged the vibrating bundle of energy while her mind whirled.

"Now, I couldn't leave her at home, could I?" a soft New Zealand voice whispered. "She hated the journey out with all the regulations, inoculations and..."

"Ray!" Bree screamed. Tears streamed from her eyes as she launched herself at the man she loved. She clung on, kissed and sobbed, kissed again and buried her head in his arms. "Ray," she wailed. "Oh my God. How..."

Ray squeezed her in a massive bear hug, then purposely ran a hand over the swell of her tummy. "You're starting to show, my sweet," he whispered.

Bree stopped and stepped back to an arm's length. "You know?" she gasped.

"Yeah, well Jenny didn't say a word but wrote a lot... email, you know."

"How long have you known?" Bree stuttered.

"A bit over three weeks."

"And neither of you said a word. My God, I'll kill her..."

"And who kept her own big secret, Bree?"

"I didn't want to pressure you." She glanced up, saw the love in her companion's eyes and slipped back into his arms.

My God, he was here, in London with her, here and now. Bree let the tears stream down and emotions take over. They were going to make it after all. They were a family. She had stretched her horizons all of the way to New Zealand, and actually made the world a smaller, and much better place.

The End

Visit the author's home page at http://www.hifiction.com

www.ingramcontent.com/pod-product-compliance
Lightning Source LLC
Chambersburg PA
CBHW060513030426
42337CB00015B/1870